Proceedings of the
Simon S. Shargo Memorial Conference

WORKING WITH REFUGEES

Proceedings of the
Simon S. Shargo Memorial Conference

WORKING WITH REFUGEES

Peter I. Rose
Editor

Smith College
Northampton, Massachusetts
March, 1983

1986
Center for Migration Studies
New York

The Center for Migration Studies is an educational non-profit institute founded in New York in 1964 to encourage and facilitate the study of sociodemographic, economic, political, historical, legislative and pastoral aspects of human migration and refugee movements. The opinions expressed in this work are those of the authors.

*Proceedings of the Simon S. Shargo Memorial Conference
(1983: Smith College)*
WORKING WITH REFUGEES

Copyright © 1986 by
The Center for Migration Studies of New York, Inc.
209 Flagg Place
Staten Island, New York 10304

Library of Congress Cataloging-in-Publication Data

Simon S. Shargo Memorial Conference
(1983: Smith College)
Working with Refugees

Includes index.
1. Refugees — Congresses.
2. Refugees — Services for Congresses.
I. Rose, Peter Isaac, 1933-
II. Title

HV640.S47 1983   362.8'7   85-47916

ISBN 0-913256-77-3 (Hardcover)
ISBN 0-913256-97-8 (Paperback)

Acknowledgements

The participants and I wish to express our gratitude to the President and Trustees of Smith College for providing a venue for this symposium, and to The Exxon Education Foundation and The Weatherhead Foundation for their financial support and encouragement.

P.I.R.

Table of Contents

Introduction	*ix*
Participants	*xii*

Proceedings of the Simon S. Shargo Memorial Conference

The Uprooted	*1*
Protection and Assistance	*10*
Selection and Admission	*29*
Resettlement	*44*
Problems of Acculturation	*61*
The Meaning of Voluntarism	*72*
Improving Services for Refugees	*83*
Retrospect and Prospect	*100*
Index	*109*

INTRODUCTION

ON March 10-12, 1983 over 100 refugee workers came to Smith College in Northampton, Massachusetts to honor the memory of Simon S. Shargo, a man most of them had never met. Yet, for all who joined us at the Shargo Memorial Conference he was a symbol, the embodiment of what "working with refugees" is all about. Simon Shargo had spent a lifetime caring for the victims of political persecution.

High officials of the United Nations High Commission for Refugees, Foreign Service Officers, adminstrators of major voluntary agencies, immigration lawyers, social workers, case managers, volunteers and several academic specialists came to discuss the protection and assistance of refugees; the rules governing their selection for relocation and the means by which they were to be admitted to "third countries" such as the United States; the initial stages of resettlement; the problems inherent in learning to adapt to a new society; and the ways services to refugees might be improved.

These subjects were considered in separate panels conducted, seriatim, over the three-day meeting. Each session had a chair who introduced the speakers and posed the problem they were to consider, several panelists, and a discussant whose remarks were often followed by further comments from those on the dais and some in the audience.

The conference opened with an introduction by Jill K. Conway, President of Smith College, and a speech by Dale DeHaan, Executive Director of the Migration and Refugee Service of Church World Service and the former Deputy High Commissioner for Refugees at the United Nations. On the second night, Sheppie Abramowitz, then the Director of the Family Liaison Unit of the State Department and former Senior Staff Member of the Khmer Emergency Group in Thailand (and the wife of Morton Abramowitz, the former Ambassador to Thailand and, later, U.S. Representative at the Conventional Arms Talks in Vienna), gave the Simon S. Shargo Memorial Lecture, speaking of the role of volunteers in crisis situations. Charles B. Keely, a demographer with the Population Council and the author of *Global Refugee Policy,* presented the final plenary address, "Retrospect and Prospect".

Those who were invited to speak were told they need not prepare formal papers in advance. The lack of formality made for a good deal of spontaniety and contributed to the liveliness of each session. It also caused difficulties (mostly minor ones) for those who read the verbatim typescripts taken from the tapes made during the conference. In addition to the common problem that unpolished speeches often have grammatical imperfections, long pauses, numerous redundancies and occasional contradictions, there was the matter of the "muted background". Reading what was said, unless one was there and can fill in with the visual and aural "memories", has significant limits. Except for occasional fiery exchanges that were recorded, the sense of atmosphere in (and outside of) the meeting rooms, the camaraderie, the tension, the raised eyebrows, the barely stifled guffaws, the warm smiles of recognition and agreement were lost.

The papers presented here have been edited but not sanitized. They are the words of the speakers, emended only to make them more readable (rather than hearable), and condensed to avoid repetition of particular ideas and pet phrases. What is still lacking is the ambience. While little can be done to capture or convey it between the covers of a collection of "Proceedings", a description may help to provide some vicarious exposure to the spirit of the conference.

Because the meeting was a tribute to Simon Shargo it was important for participants in the various sessions and members of the audience to know who he was and why we sought to honor him.

Simon Shargo was born in Nicoliev in the Ukraine on December 19, 1895, the son of a politically active father, and grandson of the *shamas* (sexton) of the largest synagogue in Odessa. Concern with oppressive regimes and with the plight of the Jewish people were family legacies that greatly influenced Simon, an agronomist and economist. From his earliest days he was involved in caring for others. In 1918 he was an assistant to the American Relief Administration in Russia administered by Herbert Hoover. Several years later he and his family, victims of persecution themselves, left their homeland forever.

In 1923 Simon joined the American Jewish Joint Distribution Committee in Germany. He served as an official of that agency working to further its triple goals of "Rescue, Relief and Reconstruction" in Berlin, Paris and Geneva for more than fifty years. Even after his formal retirement from the JDC at the age of 80, he maintained contact with thousands whose lives he had touched and continued to assist those in need.

In 1975 he moved from Geneva to Northampton, Massachusetts, the home of his daughter, Nelly Shargo Hoyt, Achilles Professor of History at Smith College and my colleague in a jointly conducted seminar on "The Experience of Exile". Simon's Northampton apartment quickly became an American version of his many European residences - a crowded port of call for old friends and new aquaintances. There Simon found time to paint, play his piano, give music lessons to neighborhood children and serve tea and pastries to his numerous guests. He also reluctantly accepted an invitation to speak to several Smith College classes about his lifelong work with refugees.

"What can I say", he would argue with me, "I'm not a teacher". But teacher he was. A spellbinder who only had to be prodded by a single query such as "Can you say something about your father's experience in Siberia?" or "What about the clandestine operations to get Jews out of Hungary?" or "What about the 'Joint's' role in providing relief to the...?" and he was off and running. He could and did provide word images of places, people and political events about which the students had read. They came alive through his discourses.

The voice of vast and varied experience was silenced on June 4, 1982 when Simon Shargo died. But many vowed to keep alive the memory of this extraordinary man, a resident of our community, and citizen of the world.

Those who came to his conference were, like those he had known and worked with, a mixed lot. There were prominent figures in international social service, including Simon's former colleagues at the JDC, directors and middle-managers of public and private agencies, church leaders and volunteers, savvy professors and sharpminded students, and several recent refugees. They met together in the sessions specified earlier and at dinners and informal gatherings, and met with students in their dormitories where lunches were arranged.

While some of the people knew each other prior to the meeting (especially a large contingent of "old Southeast Asia hands"), all seemed to feel closer at the end and, as one who wrote to Simon's daughter and to me afterwards put it, "We could feel Mr. Shargo's presence. He must have been an extraordinary man."

He was.

Peter I. Rose
Cambridge, Massachusetts
November, 1983

PARTICIPANTS*

SHEPPIE ABRAMOWITZ, *Director, Family Liaison Unit, Department of State; Former Senior Staff Member, Khmer Emergency Group, Thailand.*

GRETCHEN S. BRAINERD, *Director, Washington Office, Intergovernmental Committee for Migration.*

RICHARD BROWN, *Regional Coordinator, Lutheran Immigration and Refugee Service, Western Massachusetts; former Foreign Service Officer.*

MARGARET DYER CHAMBERLAIN, *Graduate Student, Fletcher School of Law and Diplomacy, Tufts University; Research Assistant, Smith College Study of Refugees.*

JILL K. CONWAY, *President, Smith College.*

DALE DEHAAN, *Executive Director, Migration and Refugee Program of Church World Service; former Deputy UN High Commissioner for Refugees.*

ROBERT DEVECCHI, *Deputy Director, International Rescue Committee.*

SUSAN FORBES, *Associate Director, Refugee Policy Group, Washington, D.C.*

DAVID FORD, *Deputy United States Refugee Coordinator, Department of State.*

MICHAEL FRIEDLINE, *Regional Director, World Relief, Orange County, California; Chair, Los Angeles Refugee Forum.*

LEON GORDENKER, *Professor of International Relations, Princeton University.*

MICHAEL HUYNH, *Director, Center for Southeast Asian Refugee Resettlement, San Francisco.*

---

* Affiliations listed are those held at the time of the Conference, March, 1983.

CHARLES B. KEELY, *Sociologist and Demographer, The Population Council, New York.*

STEPHANIE NEWMAN, *Director, Resource Development Department, Federation of Jewish Philanthropies, New York.*

DAVID PIERCE, *Refugee Coordinator, City Manager's Office, Orange County, California; Foreign Service Director.*

PETER POND, *Director, Refugee Resettlement for Lutheran Service Association, New England.*

MICHAEL POSNER, *Director, Lawyers Committee for Human Rights.*

JEAN PULLEN, *Director, West Portland Branch, Department of Human Resources, Portland, Oregon; Chair, Portland Refugee Consortium.*

ZIA RISVI, *Regional Representative, United Nations High Commission for Refugees, New York; formerly Coordinator, UNHCR, Southeast Asia.*

PETER I. ROSE, *Sophia Smith Professor of Sociology and Anthropology, Smith College; Conference Coordinator.*

LIONEL ROSENBLATT, *Foreign Service Officer and Una Chapman Cox Sabbatical Grantee; former U.S. Refugee Coordinator, Thailand.*

GARY RUBIN, *Associate Director, American Council of Nationalities Services.*

WILLIAM SAGE, *Director, Refugee Programs, Church World Service, Northern California; former Joint Voluntary Agency Representative, Thailand.*

MITZI SCHROEDER, *Coordinator of Overseas Programs, U.S. Catholic Conference's Migration and Refugee Service.*

BARRY STEIN, *Senior Fellow, Refugee Policy Group; Professor of Social Science, Michigan State University.*

DALE FREDERICK SWARTZ, *Director, National Immigration, Refugee, and Citizenship Forum.*

MONSIGNOR BRYAN WALSH, *Director, Catholic Community Services, Miami.*

PATRICIA WALTERMIRE, *Regional Director, Church World Service, Northern California.*

ROBYN ZIEBERT, *Pacific-American Consortium for Employment; formerly with the Intergovernmental Committee for Migration.*

NORMAN ZUCKER, *Professor of Political Science, Rhode Island University.*

KARL D. ZUKERMAN, *Executive Vice President, Hebrew Immigrant Aid Society; formerly Director, Soviet Jewish Resettlement Programs in U.S.*

THE UPROOTED

PRESIDENT Jill K. Conway: It is a pleasure and a privilege to welcome you to the Simon S. Shargo Memorial Conference, "Working with Refugees". This conference is a very special event in the life of Smith College. It commemorates a very important member of our community. It also is a conference about a theme which has enriched Smith throughout its history.

I think any historian writing about this college and its development in the twentieth century will say that it moved from being a small, quite distinguished New England college for women to becoming an institution with international aspirations and standards of scholarship very much like a university as a result of the great benefits that came to it through the movement of European intellectuals to this country, and particularly to the faculty of this college, in the late twenties and thirties. The subject of the conference is both an intimate part of our history and also an important part of our affections and ties as a community. The individual who has brought it about, Peter Rose, is a member of this faculty whose interests seem, as one looks at his life as a social scientist, always to have been tending in the direction of this subject.

This conference, funded by the college and by Weatherhead Foundation and The Exxon Education Foundation is part of the larger refugee research project at Smith, of which Mr. Rose is director.

We welcome you most warmly. While you will gain a great deal for your calling from sharing the experiences of these few days, we hope that many other generations of workers in this field will be stimulated to their first involvement as they are students here. You are very welcome, this is a proud occasion, and I am happy to introduce Peter Rose.

Peter Rose: Welcome. This is a conference on working with refugees. It is being held in memory of Simon Shargo, the father of our colleague, Nelly Hoyt. Simon was a dear friend of many of us who are here tonight and of countless thousands of people who are with us in spirit. Simon was a Russian exile who spent his entire adult life working with refugees, most of it with the American Jewish Joint Distribution Committee in Europe. He was responsible, as much as anyone, for opening my own eyes and those of many others to the complexities of rescue, relief and resettlement.

Discussing these matters with him in his apartment in Geneva and Northampton and with other people in many parts of the world, I came to realize that to deal with uprooted peoples, and to understand their needs and wants, their hopes and their fears, far too little attention is paid to those who directly and indirectly influence their lives. I refer here to the policy makers who decide what can be done about and for refugees, to the implementers of policy — from the harbormasters who control the portals to the members of government agencies — federal, state and local, to representatives of voluntary agencies and local community groups including those now ubiquitous Mutual Assistance Associations run by refugees themselves. In planning the conference every attempt was made to bring together experienced representatives of the many levels of activity that I just mentioned, and to have them (you) candidly discuss their approaches, their activities and their problems in a series of related panels.

Four such panels will be held: "Protection and Assistance", "Asylum and Admission", the initial stages of "Resettlement", and "Acculturation". Later, panelists and, hopefully, members of the audience, including representatives of various refugee groups, will discuss the issue of improving services. Sheppie Abramowitz will deliver the Shargo Memorial Lecture.

It is with considerable disappointment that I have to officially announce what you already know; Bayard Rustin was not able to come. Simon would have understood why — and I think he would have been struck by the ironic convergence of their abiding interests. At this moment Mr. Rustin is on his way to Israel for a special meeting on a subject that first concerned Simon Shargo 65 years ago: the plight of Jews under Soviet rule. While disappointed that Bayard Rustin could not be here to open the conference I am delighted to welcome a man who, perhaps more than anyone, has already played as many roles in the field of refugee work as there are statuses to occupy.

For many years, Dale DeHaan, a graduate of Georgetown and the Free University of Amsterdam, was involved in refugee work in the United States. As counsel to Senator Ted Kennedy, Mr. DeHaan was director of the Kennedy staff group that was responsible for the Refugee Act of 1980. He then became the Deputy High Commissioner for Refugees at the United Nations. His tenure in that office was marked by the number of critical decisions and involvements in the protection and assistance of millions of refugees in Southeast Asia, sub-Saharan Africa and Pakistan. He returned to the United States, leaving the international stage for what I am sure is an equally political chore of handling a voluntary agency to become the Executive Director of Immigration and Refugee Programs of Church World Service. A final demonstration of the catholicity of this representative of one of the three leading Protestant voluntary agencies is his recent acceptance of the Chair of the Committee of Migration and Refugee Affairs of the American Council of Voluntary Agencies for Foreign Service. This is the co-ordinating body of all of the volags and an important conduit through which many government policies regarding resettlement are carried out. Mr. DeHaan will address us on the subject, "The Uprooted".

Dale DeHaan: It is good to be in Massachusetts, I suppose in part because I have had a long identification with the issues and the concerns of the people in this state. But I know from my past experience that people in this Commonwealth and especially in this part of the state have a very stong interest in the kinds of things associated with refugees and other uprooted people, as well as the issues of human rights in general. I am also glad to be in this part of the state because I know that you have contributed, through the consortium of schools, to the furthering of education in many important ways and to the dissemination of public knowledge on various public issues. And I know that Smith College has played a key role in this endeavor. This conference testifies to the continuing effort and commitment on the part of this college, and this part of the Commonwealth.

I think the college and Peter Rose really deserve high tribute for organizing this conference. It is an unusual one in the sense that the organizers have sought to cover the 'waterfront', and not tried to focus on only one issue relating to refugees. They have asked the speakers and the panelists to begin with the source of the uprooted, with bringing refugees to this country, and with the various phases of their resettlement.

This kind of wholistic approach is very important in terms of helping people to understand the complexities of the issue. It is particularly fitting that we have this conference at this time because we live in a world of growing "people problems" - and declining interest in refugees and of growing neglect of the humanitarian dimension of international affairs and national foreign policies. It is fitting, as well, that the conference honors the memory of Simon Shargo, whose life and work defines the theme of this conference, "Working with Refugees", because that is where the action is and that is where it is needed today.

Speaking on "The Uprooted" is an awesome challenge. Where do you begin? Where do you end?

One thing is sure. All over the world people are on the move. Refugees. Displaced persons. Homeless people. They are people fleeing persecution and oppression; fleeing communal strife and civil war; fleeing from societies that are ravaged by tyranny and the violation of human rights; fleeing from hunger and disease.

With the help of many countries, the United Nations, the voluntary agencies, and the many private Americans who got involved, the problems in Southeast Asia have eased considerably since the time when the boats were being pushed off the shores of Malaysia. But, today, there is still a movement of people in that part of the world. That movement will continue for a long time into the future. In Africa today there are refugees from the Mediterranean Coast to the bottom of the continent. In the horn of Africa there are millions of displaced people in Ethiopia and across its borders in Somalia, the Sudan, and Djiboti. Refugees are leaving Southern Africa every day. In Namibia there are refugees. In Uganda there are homeless people and refugees. In Chad... In recent weeks, we have read about expellees from Nigeria.

Refugee problems dot the landscape, across the Muslim crescent to North Africa, to South Asia and beyond, from the western Sahara on the Atlantic to Lebanon, Iran, Iraq. There are three million Afghans in Pakistan. There are refugees from the Philippines and areas surrounding that country.

In Europe refugees continue to move from the Soviet Union, from Poland and elsewhere. The numbers today seem to be larger than they have been in the recent past. Refugees remain in Cypress today - people forget about them, but they are still there. And in our own hemisphere, in El Salvador, Nicaragua, Honduras, and Guatemala, we have a new regional crisis. There is a growing movement of people all over Central America, and the end of the turmoil there is not in sight. We don't read much about this, but there are gross violations of human rights. There probably are half a million or three quarters of a million people displaced within their own country of El Salvador. There are others in the neighboring countries. There are 300,000 El Salvadorians in this country, alone, who have fled from the oppression in their own home land. I don't know if this is a cover-up of the problems in Central America, but there is a growing tragedy there, involving individuals and families, about which very few Americans, very few people in the world, are aware. It is one thing we must look into, we must study, and try to do something about.

If we measure the state of the world by the number and scope of people movements today, of refugees, by that measure the world is in a sorry state. Refugees are a sad and tragic commentary on the state of the world because they mirror what is wrong with the world: a lack of justice, a lack of compassion, a lack of equity, a lack of better efforts to solve problems, wrong priorities, and a host of other things of which I think we are all aware.

Refugees - victims of persecution - are political pawns. They also drain the capacity for development when they move into underdeveloped areas. They impede the development of many countries. I often think of an example in Africa, where we had a kind of civil war in Chad a few years ago. Chad is in the middle of Africa, the capital is Ndjamena. There is a river which separates Chad from the neighboring country of Cameroon. Across the river from Ndjamena, there is a town called Kousseri. After a few weeks of civil war in Chad, this small community of ten thousand people was inundated with a hundred thousand refugees from its neighbor. This impeded whatever development and progress was going on in Kousseri. It used up water, it used up wood, it used up resources that were available to the people of Kousseri. I point this example out because this is happening today all over the world, and particularly in Africa and in parts of the Third World, the developing countries. This can have an enormous impact on the infrastructure which they are trying to create and on the development potential which they are trying to pursue.

When talking about refugees, the question often is, "What do we do about them?". One of the most important things that can be done for refugees, all over the world, is to protect them.

Once protected they need assistance. They need the simple, daily elements of life. They need food, clothing, shelter. They need all the kinds of things that we take for granted; the kinds of things that we call, in the refugee community, "custodial assistance" provided by voluntary agencies in cooperation with governments. There are also programs of assistance to help refugees to self-sufficiency, and to help them normalize their life to the degree they can in the areas in which they live. The most important thing, of course, is solutions for the refugee problem, that is, getting back to the source.

Solutions are needed for each group of refugees whether the Afghans in Pakistan, Cambodians in Thailand, Salvadorians in the United States - and for individuals so they can try to normalize their lives.

The United Nations does a great deal through the office of the High Commission for Refugees and through various other offices within the United Nations. A great deal is done by governments, including the U.S. government, all over the world. The voluntary agencies put in resources, funds, goods and services. They put in their commitment, they put in their diplomacy if that is required; they put in all sorts of efforts.

Politics and humanitarian needs make strange bedfellows. The humanitarian instinct tells us we have to deal with the refugees. We have to solve their problems. But, we also know that the origin of these problems is political and that, more often than not, the solution is political. Sometimes the politics of a situation does not necessarily permit a rapid resolution. So, despite the fact that much is being done, some problems last for many years. Think of the Palestinians, or the Ethiopians in Somalia. We know about Afghans in Pakistan, where there are no immediate solutions in sight.

The best solution to a problem of a refugee - whether it is a group of refugees or whether it is an individual - is to return to his country of origin, to his community: voluntary repatriation under the protection of the United Nations. The "best" solution is not always possible, but it has been that in many parts of the world. In Zimbabwe 300,000 people returned after the Independence of just a few years ago. Large numbers have returned to Cambodia, to Kampuchea, after having fled to the Thai border and to Vietnam in prior years. Many have returned to places like Sudan, and to other parts of Africa, indicating that voluntary repatriation can work. It is something we don't hear about a great deal, but it is an important alternative when we're talking about solutions to refugee problems for the individual, or for any group of refugees.

Other solutions involve settlement in the country of first asylum, as when hundred of thousands of Cubans came into this country in the early 1960s, or taking refugees from the country of first asylum to a resettlement country. The Vietnamese, Khmer, Cambodians, and Laotians have gone to Thailand, to Malaysia, to other countries in the area of Southeast Asia, to find temporary asylum. Various programs of the United Nations, local governments and voluntary agencies have provided protection and assistance and [prepared] them for resettlement in the United States, Australia, Canada, and various countries of Europe.

As the late poet Robert Lowell said, "The world is tired". Perhaps it is true. But it is not the kind of attitude that is going to solve problems, either today or in the future. So what do we do about refugees?

There is a great debate going on these days about "root causes". This is a very important area. But in some quarters, a focus on "root causes", on trying to deal with the violation of human rights, with bad economic conditions, with tyrannies, and all the other things that create refugees, while important, can be a figleaf for action. And action is needed.

What more can we do if we don't just focus on "root causes"? Well, we can talk about what more can be done in the international community. The focus here is on the United Nations.

There is no better forum in the world today to deal with these people problems, and perhaps with the political problems which surround various issues in Asia, Africa and elsewhere. The United Nations can help neutralize the political context in which a problem exists. There is a proven record that the United Nations can do a great deal in order to help refugees and bring about solutions to the problem. But, I think, given the nature of the problems we have in the world, the kinds of problems that we have to deal with, and the fact that we don't have one crisis today but multiple crises all over the world, the United Nations is not doing enough. I don't think they are living up to the needs in either the humanitarian context or the political context. What we need more of, in the international arena, is leadership. We need more creativity, we need more initiative. We have to take the risk within the international community to try to bring about new approaches to refugee problems.

We can't get too argumentative about whether or not a certain group of people falls under the mandate, under the duties, or under the responsibilities of any particular United Nations agency. We went through that during the Nigerian Civil War and the Pakistani Civil War. I think today, at a time when we are having new kinds of problems and new kinds of pressures brought about by the violations of human rights and the movement of people in the world, we need new efforts within the United Nations, and new approaches to try to deal with humanitarian problems.

Perhaps we - I am throwing out some ideas here, I don't have answers to all these questions - need some review of the definition of a refugee. We need a review of the mandates and the prescribed and understood responsibilities of the office of the United Nations High Commission for Refugees, and perhaps other offices within the United Nations. We need more structural coalescence, more coordination, more efficiency which gets to the point of leadership within the United Nations family. We also need a new approach to the permanent solutions of refugee problems which threaten to go on year after year after year.

New approaches can be taken to help solve these problems. There were many problems during the 1970s - new problems - and initiatives were taken within the United Nations with the support of governments. Progress was made in the solutions of these problems. Even in recent years, there were international conferences convened by the Secretary General to deal with specific kinds of problems. There was a conference of governments on Southeast Asia refugees in 1979. There was a conference called by the Secretary General on refugees in Africa in 1981. New approaches were taken in trying to negotiate with governments the orderly departure of people from Vietnam, to help avoid their taking the boats. These things don't solve problems, but they represent new approaches within the structure of the United Nations, if not their final solution. So, I repeat again: there is only one place within the international community where many refugee-related problems can really be dealt with in an appropriate way - the United Nations.

On a national basis all countries can do a great deal more. In the United States we have had a bi-partisan consensus in the last generation on how to deal with refugees - both overseas and in this country. But I am troubled. I share the view of those who believe that this consensus is withering away. It is crumbling. It may be the function of the economy. It may also be the function of new approaches to government. Whatever the cause, the kind of consensus that has existed since the Second World War, under many administrations through the '50s, '60s and '70s, is changing. It is hurting refugees. It is hurting our national commitment to refugees. It is hurting the moral basis on which this commitment is based.

In Cambodia today (I don't want to get too technical here for we will be talking about admission and selection practices later) it should be stated that a number of people have returned from being displaced on the Thai border and elsewhere. Over the past few years, they have been helped to rehabilitate their lives by the support of the U.S., by the support of American voluntary agencies. There are American voluntary agencies there today who are helping these people to repair their lives. But my point is that on the other side of the border, in Thailand, there are also some Cambodians. These people have chosen not to return to their homeland, for whatever reason. And they are being rejected. They are being turned down for admission to the United States even though they may have family members here, even though they have every right to fear persecution upon return to their communities. They are being turned down not because there aren't any numbers for these people. The Congress has authorized 64,000 numbers for the admission of Indochinese refugees. The President of the United States has proclaimed that 64,000 Indochinese refugees can come into this country. We have sponsors in this country. We have people who want to help refugees: individuals, congregations, parishes, what-have-you. But, our national policy - or what there is of it - seems to say "No, we are closing the door on you. We don't need you. We don't want you. We are rejecting you." By the same token, within this country, we have thousands and thousands of refugees. People who have fled civil wars in El Salvador and elsewhere. People who have left Haiti for fear of persecution or because they were persecuted. The policy of our government today, at least in part, is to throw these people in the "pokey", and to leave them there without any - or with very few - rights. Litigation is necessary to deal with their claims, to get them any hearing, while the rest are ignored.

One of the major issues today, in this country, is that of the asylum-seeking undocumented aliens, those who really are refugees or who claim refugee status - people who need temporary safe haven because of events in their home country. But, we don't have a policy to deal with them, except to ignore them. And, if we can deport them, that is what we do.

We can and should provide a formula whereby people who come to this country and claim asylum or claim refugee status or claim a status of temporary safe haven can have their interests accomodated instead of letting them walk the streets in fear, becoming part of a sub-rosa society in which they don't really contribute much good to the community at large. We have found these formulas before - it is easy to do - but the will to do it must be there.

On the question of resettlement of refugees: many who are brought to this country from Southeast Asia, from Europe, Afghans from Pakistan and elsewhere, Ethiopians, South Africans, Soviet Jews, Poles and others, and many who work with them don't really know what the policy of our government is. The consensus has crumbled. We hear one thing one day, and one thing another day. We will continue to resettle refugees, I am sure of that. But what we need today, in the times in which we live, is some national leadership of the kind that we have had in the past, and the kind that we should continue to have today and in the future.

What can we do? We can work on the international arena; we can try to get better things going in this country. And we as individual citizens, people concerned with refugees - whether experts, practitioners, or interested citizens, or students - can advocate. We can try to create a public opinion on these issues. I think that is what we really have to do.

There is a great deal to do in the field of refugees. It is an important area of public policy, and it is a crucial issue for our country and the world. We have an obligation and a responsibility, as individuals, as a people, and as a country to help insure a better sense of compassion, justice and common human decency in our national policy. We have many problems here at home. We have homeless people in the streets. We have uprooted people in our country. But, if we claim to be leaders in the world community, then I think we have to try to balance our responsibilities and our efforts. We must help people at home, obviously. But we must also help people overseas. Perhaps the world cannot outlaw war. Perhaps it cannot outlaw the violation of human rights. But, we can all help make the world just a little bit more civilized.

As Albert Camus put it many years ago, "Perhaps we cannot prevent this world from being a world in which children are tortured, but we can reduce the number of tortured children".

And if you don't help, who else in the world can help us do this?

Peter Rose: Thank you, Dale. I think you have given us a good deal of food for thought.

PROTECTION AND ASSISTANCE

Leon Gordenker: Dale DeHaan referred to the coming and going of refugees, of people who know about refugees, and the likelihood that they would encounter each other. I am very amused to find that this panel, for the most part, has already had a go at each other at a conference on Cambodia that was held at Princeton University on the initiative of a of a group of students. Their performance was extraordinary for three reasons. First, they have experience. Second, they are interested in communicating that experience. The third is perhaps the most important one of all: they really care about those people who are in the status of refugees, who are forced migrants and whose future is so delicately balanced. The panelists will speak briefly, then have a chance, after Bob DeVecchi sums up and takes a general look at what is being said, to come back at each other. And, if by some miracle - no, if by some feat of self-discipline - there is still time left, then I will invite questions from the audience.

That being said, let me introduce Barry Stein, Professor of Social Science at Michigan State University. He is a pioneer in the academic study of refugee questions and now a Senior Associate with the Refugee Policy Group in Washington. I think he will give particular attention to refugees - forced migrants in the poorer parts of the world.

Barry Stein: Thank you Lee.

I want to deal with the question of assistance to refugees in developing countries. It is my understanding that much of the conference will deal with resettlement, so I want to deal with just about everything but resettlement.

It is important to note that approximately 90 percent of the world's refugees (and we variously count refugees at about 10 to 18 million depending upon what year it is) are from the less developed countries. That's where most of the origin of refugee movements is. More importantly, over 90 percent of all refugees will stay in developing countries.

Very few will be resettled. For calendar year 1983 it is unlikely that worldwide resettlement will total some place between 100,000 and 150,000. It is a small part of the overall 10-18 million refugees.

The three things that happen to most refugees is: they are repatriated, going back to their homelands; they are integrated in the country of first asylum, the country to which they have fled; or, the classic nonsolution, they linger in some kind of temporary status, in some kind of limbo, in refugee camps or in some kind of unsure legal status.

Refugees who stay in the less-developed countries are aided by those countries. We quite often talk about the huge burden on the U.S. and the other donor countries, but a large share of the costs for refugees are borne by the host governments themselves. Also of importance with regard to refugees in the developing countries is the fact that most of the refugees, the overwhelming majority, are from rural areas and they will stay in rural areas in their sanctuary. So, we're talking about refugees in the poorest countries, and generally in the poorest parts of the poorest countries. Most of the large refugee movements right now are occurring not just in less-developed countries, but in the least developed of the less-developed countries, in countries that make the World Bank's "Poorest Country List".

Despite what everybody says, the continent with the largest number of refugees is not Africa, it is Asia. Asia has about 5 million refugees. Africa has about 2.5 million; Latin America and Central America have about one-half million. That number may be doubled or tripled if displaced persons are added, people who have not crossed international boundaries (actually you can have little faith in any of the numbers that are generally given as the counting is usually extremely difficult and extremely iffy).

There has been a change in the character of Third World refugee problems in recent years. The key change is in the causes of the problems. For the most part, through the '50s, '60s and into the '70s, the main cause of refugee movements was independent struggle from European colonial rule. When there was that kind of refugee movement, there was a certain solidarity in the sanctuaries, solidarity in the host countries - and within the refugee population there was also a sense that at a certain point the tide of history was on your side. It might take five years, it might take twenty years, but you were going to win your independence and the refugee problem would be solved in its ultimate by repatriation. What we are now seeing is a new kind of refugee movement in the developing countries, a much less tractable kind of movement.

One shouldn't predict and speculate, but everybody should be taking some early warning signs by the fact that Joshua Nkomo has left Zimbabwe. He is one refugee, but he could be the harbinger of 100,000 refugees from that country. Just a few years ago we had several hundred thousand Zimbabwe refugees. Then Zimbabwe became independent and the refugees went home. Now what is happening, and Zimbabwe would be the sign of it, is not white against black, it is not external to Africa, but it is internal within the country. It is tribe against tribe, ethnic group against ethnic group, economic group against economic group. The oppressor is native to the area. And so, what you have is the problem in many refugee situations now: "They ain't going home". The refugees are less likely to repatriate, or if they will repatriate they will do so after an extremely long delay. Thus the need, the problem has changed in its character. We cannot be so easily sure that the refugees will go home: more likely they will stay in their country of first asylum. Since the cause is different, there is likely to be less solidarity from the hosts; less interests in helping.

If refugees are not going to go home, if they are going to be out longer, then we have to start to alter the way we assist them especially those in developing countries. In the past, if we thought they were going home, we gave them care and maintenance relief. Temporary measures were provided to take care of them until repatriation occurred. Now it seems those costs may just go on and on and on, for they do not move back.

It is now being argued that the refugees must be integrated into the development program of the host country. Ways must be found to have a transition from relief to self-sufficiency or self-reliance. We must have ways to help plan the phase-out of assistance.

We are now hearing a term, originally from Senator Simpson, of the "compassion fatigue" of donor countries because they are not interested in paying the costs of relief over an endless, open-ended time period. What is needed, in terms of developing country refugees, is much more attention, very early in a refugee emergency, to the question of whether or not those refugees are likely to be repatriated soon. And, if they are not likely to be repatriated, then it is necessary to move into a development kind of scheme as quickly as possible.

I say this with full understanding of the political problems of host countries that absolutely cannot admit to their own population that these refugees will not go home. This is a new area, and a very difficult area to work in, but what we're talking about is timing: moving as quickly as possible not necessarily to the most desirable solution, but to the most available solution. And so, this is the problem with refugees in developing countries.

Leon Gordenker: Our next speaker is Lionel Rosenblatt, a Foreign Service Officer who served in Southeast Asia and was directly involved with the movement of refugees out of Thailand into permanent asylum. He was therefore intimately connected with trying to understand how those refugees got there. As former Refugee Coordinator in Thailand for the U.S. government, he also was at a kind of junction point of policy and administration. He is currently Una Chapman Cox Sabbatical Grantee, in the Department of State, which means that he has been welcomed, temporarily, to the ranks of the researchers, and works at the Refugee Policy Group in Washington.

Lionel Rosenblatt: I am in the happy position of being able to say that, thanks to the Una Chapman Cox program, I am speaking totally for myself, and certainly not for either the U.S. government or the RPG (Refugee Policy Group). I am going to try to look at some of the key lessons that I feel we learned from the Indochinese refugee experience, both in the temporary asylum aspects and the failure of the temporary asylum upon occasion (most notably in 1979), and then the kinds of 'durable solutions', as the UNHCR terms runs, for refugees in temporary asylum: what are the preferred outcomes and how can we stimulate more movement toward final outcomes, rather than simple care and maintenance in camps.

My sabbatical year is concentrated on the links between the domestic and foreign policy aspects of refugees. I think that it is axiomatic but often forgotten that how well this country does on resettlement of refugees, in Santa Ana or in St. Paul, is going to greatly affect our ability to respond to the international aspects of crises down the line. When a Congressman hears about a refugee issue - it may be some group in Africa having nothing to do with Indochinese or Cubans in his own backyard - that Congressman is first going to view refugees through his own narrow prism: "What do I know about refugees?" "Are my constitutents angry about refugee matters for one reason or another?" So, what happens at the grass roots, how we can improve resettlement, how we can make it more cost effective, how we can bring people to self-sufficiency earlier bears very directly on our future ability to respond to the international crisis which we can anticipate. Having said that the domestic situation can fundamentally influence how much aid and how much generosity we exhibit towards crises, let's look at the basic fundamental of an international refugee crisis: to make sure that first asylum is maintained. That is, that there is a refuge for fleeing refugees, and that they are not pushed back from that refuge. In other words, *non-refoulement* as the legal term goes.

Basically, protection against involuntary repatriation is the most fundamental of the rights which refugees are accorded by the convention, and which we must all work together to buttress. The notable failure in the Indochinese context came in 1979 when the boat refugees were pushed off-shore chiefly by the Malaysians, but also [by] some of the other governments in the area. At the same time (much less noticed because it was much less traumatic and much less newsworthy), thousands of Khmer were sent back into Cambodia over a cliff in the northeast section of Thailand.

The denial of first asylum, the forced repatriation of refugees, costs lives. Everything we do ought to be premised to prevent those kinds of enormous human rights violations from occurring. The lesson from the Indochinese experience was that resettlement was the key ingredient towards maintaining temporary asylum.

Very early on, as Indochinese fled, the assurances from the United States and other countries that these Indochinese would be resettled was what kept this framework alive. When the flow of refugees began to exceed the ability of the resettlement countries to respond rapidly, the countries of temporary asylum figured out how to catch the international community's eyes, and refugees were simply turned away.

One could argue that maybe there ought to have been a different basis for the temporary asylum framework, but there wasn't. Trying to get people to see that very simple linkage came, for those of us in the field, too little, too late. Governments like that in Thailand did basically ask the U.S. and other countries: "What are you going to do? Our neighbor Cambodia is hemorrhaging and we're left with the prospect that there may be millions of people seeking sanctuary in our country. What can you do?"

Our response, until June of 1979, was to shrug our shoulders. We sympathized, but we were unable to make commitments. Oddly enough, in June of 1979 the U.S. government came up with a very generous Indochinese resettlement program of 14,000 a month, leading the international community into the Geneva conference. It was still too little, too late. The private sector needs to play a much more vigorous advocacy role.

When you have a problem such as this developing, and the press in particular is not picking it up, the private sector has a role to play. The IOs - international organizations - and the governments -the normal institutions - tend to be rather cautious, sluggish. Unless there is a private sector effort to galvanize the attention of the world, this kind of pattern is going to be repeated. Refugees don't often make the news until the worst has happened.

Consider the approach with Cambodians. From the ashes of involuntary repatriation, thanks in large measure to U.S. government pressure, a new Thai policy emerged, an open door policy towards refugees. Actually, we were making things up as we went along - not just we in the U.S. government side, but also, UNHCR, UNICEF, and the ICRC (the International Committee of the Red Cross). What fundamentally happened is that, rather than simply letting the Cambodian refugees wander into Thailand refugee camps, provisions were made by ICRC and UNICEF (again too late in my view) to house, shelter and maintain refugees along the border. This turned out to be a very wise decision, although it has cost refugees in terms of fatalities from time to time because of lack of security. Remarkably, most of the Khmer managed to survive and repatriate. They never broke their nexus with their country. That is important because we didn't need a formal voluntary repatriation program. Many Cambodians, when they felt safe, were able to go back. The idea of a temporary refugee zone, contiguous with the origin country's border, that permits spontaneous decisions to return is something we ought to look at as a precedent for the future. That is a way out of the present situation where people enter the camps and then years later decide to repatriate or resettle.

There were some Khmer who, from the beginning, chose not to stay on the border, despite the availability of care and feeding. They moved into the holding centers in Thailand run by the UNHCR. One of the problems we had was that there was not a single overall mandate. ICRC and UNICEF were along the border, and UNHCR was inside Thailand. That led to a certain lack of coordination. UNHCR very successfully and quickly put up and ran holding centers in Thailand, centers that housed 160,000 Cambodians. The outcome for most of those in the camps has now been determined. Twenty to thirty thousand voluntarily went back to the border, from there presumably on into Cambodia. Others have been resettled. It is the residue that is of concern - the residue that all of us told the Thai government they would not be left with now consists of 40-50,000 Cambodians, the most vulnerable case load in all of the Indochina scene.

What has happened there, I'm afraid, is that the resettlement interest waned before the problem was solved. We all approached the Khmer differently, and decided the Khmer would not be allowed - even those who came into the holding centers - to move into the resettlement stream early. Let them sit, think about going back, voluntary repatriation was something that ought to be tried first, an approach to which I heartily subscribe. What happened is that as this has been tried, and so far unsuccessfully, the interest of the international resettlement community has waned. Each year we have had to go back and carve out new numbers once again for Cambodians who don't ever quite come in a given year. This leads to the suggestion that maybe we need a multi-year approach to refugee admissions. We need to insure that when commitments are made to governments about resettlement levels, there is some way of following through. Again, UNHCR has a role to play, governments have a role to play. But, the private sector needs to have a long memory on problems such as these.

Those are the key lessons. We've got to go back to basics. With resources stretched thin, with refugee populations growing around the world, let us remember the fundamental obligation is to try to make sure that people, refugees, have a right of free choice, are given refuge when needed, and are not pushed back involuntarily.

Leon Gordenker: When refugees move from camps to permanent asylum, they have to be under the tutelage of something and someone. Our next speaker, Robyn Ziebart, can tell us a good deal about providing that link and the process of bringing refugees to a kind of permanent asylum. Robyn Ziebart was formerly an official of an organization which is practically unknown, but has been around and has moved millions of people since the early 1950s. This is the Intergovernmental Committee for Migration. She represented them in the field in Southeast Asia and also in the U.S. in connection with the Cuban flow. She is currently at PACE, the Pacific Asian Consortium for Employment, in the California area. This is an organization which is devoted to integrating new immigrants and former refugees into American society.

Robyn Ziebert: I am going to address another issue in refugee protection and assistance. I think that we have a very limited view in the U.S. of refugee assistance. To most of us it means resettlement. We also think of large numbers of people fleeing boundaries and seeking asylum. As mentioned before, protection and assistance means rescue, relief and durable solutions. There is a myriad of agencies which carry out those tasks including the United Nations High Commissioner for Refugees, other U.N. agencies, the voluntary agencies, private relief organizations and some international, intergovernmental agencies such as ICM. ICM, originally the Intergovernmental Committee for European Migration, was established in 1952 to carry out the operational aspects of refugee assistance and to facilitate the movement of displaced persons. ICM itself is essentially a technical, nonpolitical agency which deals with people regardless of whether they are officially considered under the international definition of a refugee. And, as I said, one of its main objectives is to aid in the processing and in the movement of those people to countries offering them legal resettlement opportunities.

Some of the notable examples of ICM-assisted programs have been the movement of the White Russians from the People's Republic of China to Australia, to the U.S. and to other countries offering them resettlement opportunities since the early '50s. ICM has moved Asians out of Uganda and has taken care of Hungarians in 1956, Chileans in the '70s and, more recently, Palestinians, when they left Lebanon. It has also been of primary importance in Southeast Asia in processing and moving refugees.

ICM is responsible for many things that take place prior to admittance to a new country. There are papers and documents to be prepared; there are medical examinations; there are transportation arrangements to be made. It takes a good deal of time, effort and many people in the field. ICM staff members work in coordination with voluntary agencies, the UNHCR and the agencies in the countries of first asylum as well as the third countries of resettlement.

In some cases, movement and processing takes place in a very orderly fashion. It is planned in anticipation of what is going to happen. In other cases there is little time to prepare.

For example, there were movements of large troop transports, called LSTs, to the Philippines from Thailand, Malaysia and Hong Kong. The first ship came from Thailand. It was an emergency effort to transport Cambodians from Thailand to the Philippines and it occurred at the time when there was an imminent attack across the Thai border. They had to move Cambodians from that area.

Another instance of ICM's involvement in movement was during the Mariel boatlift period. It was quite unique in U.S. history. We had dealt with large scale influxes of Cuban refugees in the 1960s and with those fleeing Vietnam after the fall of Saigon in 1975. However, again, those were planned - at least to some extent. Soon after ICM first began to handle the flights out of the Peruvian embassy in Havana, negotiations broke down and the Mariel boatlift occurred. Refugees began coming in droves to the U.S. and someone had to be there to help coordinate the transportation, getting them from Key West, getting them from Miami, from Eglin AFB, etc., to their relatives in Miami and other parts of Florida, or getting them up to the camps in Fort Indiantowngap, Fort McCoy and Fort Chaffee. Processing centers were established in those camps to process, release and resettle refugees as orderly and quickly as possible. Again, ICM assisted in coordination with many other agencies.

Refugee work, protection and assistance, again, does not just mean movement and asylum. It also means assistance at the local level. Recently I have been running a large scale employment program in California, an impacted area. Of primary importance for refugees when they come to a new country is the attainment of self-sufficiency. We have to move them off welfare rolls, help them to integrate into our society and assist them in finding employment. That is where a lot of money is going at this point in time. I think it is important to keep in mind that those are the kinds of things to which we have to pay most attention.

Employment means finding job situations for refugees, developing their skills, dealing with removing the barriers to opportunity - which are multitudinous - and assisting them in their adjustment in terms of orientation, ESL and vocational training. We are looking at direct placement for refugees. It is a common fallacy that most refugees are on welfare, that they are on the 'dole', and that they are lazy. That is not true. There are a great many refugees who want to achieve self-sufficiency and are looking for jobs. They need assistance. We need more creative ways to develop programs for employment for refugees.

Leon Gordenker: I think you can see from the comments so far that we're dealing with a very long process when we talk about the ultimate resolution of refugee incidents. There is a tangle of organizational relationships and governmental decisions which, of course, involves humanitarian issues and a great deal more.

Our next speaker has been at one of the nerve junction points for this vast network of agencies, and of activities that extend from the grass roots of Los Angeles to the meetings of the majestic diplomats every year as they decide on the future of those millions out there.

Zia Risvi, a Pakistani jurist, has been the Executive Assistant to the UNHCR, the head of the UNHCR's office in Rome. He was the coordinator for the UNHCR in Southeast Asia, and is now the regional representative of the UNHCR at U.N. headquarters in New York. He has responsibilities for the U.S. and the Caribbean. He will probably - if I may anticipate one issue that I'd like him to talk about - explain how decisions on humanitarian assistance are made.

Zia Risvi: This morning I got lost. I didn't known which way I should go. That mentally prepared me for talking about refugees.

I won't speak as a U.N. official. I'll talk about politics. I hope my statement will be less boring if I speak in a personal capacity.

"Working with Refugees" - the title inspired me. The key word is "empathy"; to feel as a refugee does.

I have worked now almost half my life for and with refugees. I feel a personal failure in large response to refugee problems, both in terms of assistance and protection. When Dale DeHaan was talking about politics of the refugee business, I was reminded of a British political joke in the time of Harold Wilson. One of the speakers said: "There are two things I don't like about Harold Wilson. His face." Refugees today are being dealt with in the same way. There is the politics of humanitarianism, and there is humanitarian politics. And these two things together, these two faces, interact and produce results which are not satisfactory.

From the part that I heard earlier, I felt very tempted to take this debate out of the United States, not because it is not pertinent to the United States - it is very much. Nations are preoccupied with their own problems. When they start thinking about economics, when they start believing that foreign policy is exclusively an extension of internal politics, when they believe that national trusts must come first whatever happens in the world, a number of good things may happen to the country concerned, but one thing certainly also happens as far as humanitarianism is concerned - it suffers.

The refugees are suffering today. We are becoming poorer in finding solutions and richer in problems because their number is increasing. In fact, we are now at a state where we don't even know "who" is a refugee. This is where I will consider the question of protection.

There is considerable confusion now. To arouse sympathy one may talk about 10 million refugees, about children, about piracy, rape and so on. And the matter stays there. Of course, working with refugees is a matter of feeling more than anything else. But it is of utmost importance that the problems are approached in perceptual terms - in terms of thinking - because as far as protection is concerned, international legislation, international thinking on the problem is lagging way behind history, behind our times. We haven't found any new approach, any new solution to the problem since the Second World War.

In terms of assistance, again we haven't shown, in the last two or three decades, any ingenuity. From time to time there are fits of humanitarianism generosity, sometimes an overzealous attitude towards one particular problem. We always end up doing either too much or too little, and both are bad for the human being. Doing too much impairs the dignity of the person concerned, his initiative. Doing too little doesn't take him very far. And I wouldn't limit this discussion to Southeast Asia, even though I am very influenced by my work there. In some areas there was too much done there and in other areas there was too little.

Take, first, protection. In the refugee business we learn the art of giving the benefit of doubt. So, I'll give benefit of doubt to everybody in terms of the Convention.

In the case of refugees, for example, there are several categories that have emerged for whom no particular terms and no particular legislation exists: displaced persons; economic migrants; illegal aliens; victims of civil strife and civil war. In the United Nations, when we talk about refugees, we talk essentially about people who have left their country for another country for reasons of persecution or well founded fear of persecution. What happens when a country gets divided? For all practical purposes, it remains one country legally. An example is Vietnam. It was divided into two countries for many, many years. The constitution of both parts of Vietnam proclaimed Vietnam to be one country. So, when people left North Vietnam and went to South Vietnam, they were in their own country; they weren't refugees. But for all practical purposes, they were refugees. Laotians had the same thing - the Pathet Lao controlling two thirds of the country and the royal side, one third; people moving from one part to the other, still in their own country. There was no way, in terms of the law - refugee law - that we could apply the term 'refugee' to these situations. So, we came up with the rather vague term of 'displaced persons', which was used in a very different context after the Second World War - displaced person who were displaced by war, and so on.

In the Third World, in Africa particularly, Nigeria and Uganda come to mind. People are talking more and more of economic migrants, illegal aliens, and of those who are undesirable and who should, at a given stage of a country's economy, go home. In many of these situations, in physical and mental terms, these people suffer almost as much as refugees. There is a very scarce amount of legislation on the rights of aliens or of foreign workers.

Victims of civil war are also similar to refugees. If there is trouble in a country and one part, one minority, or one area of the country suffers some displacement of the population which moves to the other part of the country, for all practical purposes they have left their homes. They have cut their ties with whatever they were. I have seen that in Lebanon for many years before Southeast Asia. They are totally like refugees, but they aren't considered refugees.

Considering legislation on protection of victims of civil conflicts, of struggles for liberation in certain areas, naturally one can think of the International Red Cross and the Geneva Convention. But there are many areas for protection of such categories which are not covered yet by conventions. Somehow humanity makes progress in the humanitarian field only when there is a tragedy, a shock, as though a war is needed in order to elaborate humanitarian principles. Since World War II we haven't moved more than two steps on legislation. In fact, in the United Nations when we tried to change and adjust our definitions, say about territorial asylum or about refugees, the states went backwards instead of moving forwards. They were much more restrictive in their approach than liberal as one would have expected. And, amazingly, the more an individual today, in the context of human rights, asserts his position, the more the states become tyrannical about human rights and about individuals. It is the classic conflict between the 'monists' and the 'dualists' of international law, the position of the individual and the position of the state. But beyond that, more and more, even in countries which are democracies like the U.S., human rights is a problem. In that area generally, and specifically when dealing with displaced persons and refugees, there is work to do in terms of protection.

There are now problems of international protection versus actual protection of refugees. When we say protection of refugees we tend to mean international protection, which is protecting them against *refoulement* (being sent back), against expulsion, and so. What happens if the refugee comes to a country, as they often do, in the Third World where the nationals of the country are not adequately protected? Or, where the country of asylum has a government which has rather a restrictive attitude towards refugees? Or, where the country of asylum is a government which has a rather restrictive attitude towards refugees and there is a problem of physical security of refugees? Of course, the United Nations wouldn't physically go and protect the refugees in their country of asylum; they would just ask the country of asylum to be nice towards them. But the problem is becoming very real. Very often, the refugees themselves, people who work for refugees and those who want to work for refugees wonder what the United Nations is doing. These refugees, poor devils, are being slaughtered. They are being kidnapped.

There is nothing in international legislation; there is nothing in the powers attributable to the United Nations by governments to extend such protection. It is essentially the work of the governments of the countries of asylum. When they misbehave, well, where do you go? Particularly when, in continents like Africa, the countries are exporters and importers of refugees at the same time. Who is going to throw the first stone at whom? The problem becomes very serious.

Assistance was conceived at the beginning of UNHCR more as a means to an end. The end was permanent solutions. As we got into the '60s and '70s and into Africa and Asia, and generally the Third World, the means have become the end: 'relief'. That is the end of the story. You just perpetuate the problem. There are countries that have had refugees for twenty years and nobody is able to say "naturalize them or integrate them. They aren't refugees any more". Because in the Third World there are economic needs, countries want to have as many sources of aid as possible. And relief has become a thing in itself - an end in itself. I don't mean to criticize any particular country, but this is generally the attitude. Of course, the do-gooders, the donors, are able to buy time and are able to respond to public outcry by being quite selective and giving here and there, not in order to cure, but just in order to keep it going, to keep a lid on. The net result: there are no solutions to refugee problems.

In the last two decades, except in the case of voluntary repatriation - which was a political matter, not humanitarian in most cases - there haven't been any political solutions. In the last twenty years the six or seven major operations of voluntary repatriation have been essentially because the process was preceded by agreements between governments. Without them, the U.N. can try as hard as possible, but unless the climate exists, the political will exists, the willingness of the country of origin and the country of asylum exists and therefore an agreement exists (like that relating to the Sudanese return, or the Delhi agreement about the Bangladesh return), one can go on trying hard. I tried hard with regard to the Kampuchea. It was not because I had any illusions that there was going to be a great agreement, but essentially so that there is a climate that is created and that there is an illusion then. We live in illusions: not only refugees, but generally speaking. So we buy time; we just buy time...

Leon Gordenker: I think I'd like to buy some time from you now. If you stop here we'll get back to what you are saying. Thank you very much.

I'm going to ask Bob DeVecchi to comment on all of what we've heard. Like everybody on this panel, Robert DeVecchi brings direct experience with refugee situations to us. Since 1972, he has been part of the staff of the International Rescue Committee, of which he is now Deputy Director. The IRC is one of the oldest of the voluntary agencies that has worked with refugees. Before that he was, among other things, a member of the United States Foreign Service.

Robert DeVecchi: Thank you. Your mentioning the hoary age of the IRC leads into one of the things that I wanted to say which I am not sure is the prerogative of a discussant. That is, that it is interesting with such a distinguished panel that two aspects have not been mentioned. One has been the extraordinary movement of refugees from Europe to the United States starting in the post-war period. I was thinking to myself, what would Simon Shargo be thinking if he were here, and not hear about mention made of the University-in-Exile; what has happened to the academic community; how the artistic movement, the abstract expressionist movement and how modern music was altered; how so many things that we take for granted, in terms of the U.S. being the 'center' of where it's happening, as the cultural wellspring of the Western world, is the result of refugees, and the result of refugees from Western Europe in the period of the 1930s on.

Actually, this is for my agency a rather historic month because it was exactly fifty years ago, one week after Adolf Hitler became Chancellor of Germany, that the Emergency Rescue Committee was established by Albert Einstein and Eleanor Roosevelt. We were a subversive organization. We were illegally sneaking people out of Europe and in some cases sneaking them into the United States. So, to be sitting on the same panel with a Foreign Service Officer who should technically be arresting me shows how far we have come.

Secondly, I think another point that has not surfaced here, which is one that perhaps we unconsciously or maybe even consciously try to repress, is the fact that the U.S., for better or for worse, has become a major country of first asylum. We have some very serious problems wrestling with our own conscience in terms of how we handle first asylum refugees. It is very easy to sit back and wave our finger at the Thais, or to castigate the Malaysians for pushing boats off, but as Monsignor Walsh in particular, who is here from Miami and who is perhaps the most experienced person in this field, can certainly bear better witness than I, the U.S. is now a country of first asylum. And, what are the implications of that?

Every indication is that this is not a passing phenomenon, but indeed, with the turbulence in Central America, with the continuing economic and political strife in the Caribbean area, the U.S. will have increasing problems in dealing with first asylum which, up to this point, we have dealt with mainly by putting people in detention and forcing them back, or by allowing them to 'disappear' into our society and pretend we have a control on something over which we frankly do not have any control. This is a matter I hope will come up later in this meeting with others like Rick Swartz who are infinitely more knowledgeable on these issues. What are the rights of the undocumented alien, the Haitians, the Mariel Cubans, the Salvadorian refugees? Right now I am sure, a plane is being loaded in California someplace where Salvadorans who have been begging for political asylum are being sent back to El Salvador.

But, to return to the panel and the discussion, I found a very interesting theme I would like to throw out and have the panelists discuss with each other.

We have traditionally thought of the three classic solutions to refugee emergencies: repatriation; local integration; or resettlement in the third country.

Barry Stein led off by pointing out that perhaps there are situations that have evolved particularly in the Third World, markedly in Africa (but certainly Cambodia could be considered a similar situation) where there are large numbers of people who are not candidates for resettlement, who are refusing repatriation, and who are temporarily in a country or on the border of a country that has said they cannot stay. To me, this is one of the most intriguing new aspects of the refugee dilemma, and one that I would be most anxious to have the panelists discuss. Is there a new aspect? As Lionel Rosenblatt tried to put in some concrete form, is the Cambodian border operation the wave of the future? As Africa goes into a post-colonial phase, and more and more internal problems along tribal and cultural lines begin to emerge so that the traditional hospitality from one African country to another begins to dribble away, can we expect new challenges of large movements of people for whom one of the three solutions simply do not exist? I think the ICM has a major role to play in trying to define some of these new areas, too.

It's curious, again, the evolution, and I here was thinking of Mr. Shargo. ICM used to be called "I-C-E-M", the Intergovernmental Commission for European Migration. It wasn't until two years ago that the 'European' was dropped. Its name recognizes what it has been for a long time, and that is a world-wide organization that not only has been seeking to facilitate the movement of refugees, but also has developed imaginative and creative programs such as the return of talent and the assisting of Third World countries - assisting skilled people who are unable to find their niche in their developed society to go to a society where their skills are desperately needed.

I would be interested in having the panelists explore the question of, "Is there a fourth solution to refugee problems?" Or, "Is there a fourth problem developing?" If so, how do we define the parameters and how should a lead country, such as the U.S., respond in terms of seeking durable solutions that don't meet the convenient definitions we have all gotten used to using.

Leon Gordenker: Thank you very much. I am going to ask the panel to comment on each other's statements, or on Bob DeVecchi's statement, or to bring in anything more they would like. But, before I do that I cannot let go an occasion to throw in some of my own words.

One line that surely has emerged from this whole discussion is the doubt about what the international norm is with regard to refugees. Since 1945, when as a very young man I was asked to write a pamphlet about the displaced persons that the U.N. Relief and Rehabilitation Administration was trying to care for in Europe, I have realized there are many more people in the world and a great deal more destructive capacity in the hands of a great many more governments who may or may not recognize that there are some norms of behavior. Related to that is my bemusement with the question of whether there has been a retrogression on the ability of governments to settle disputes among themselves. Certainly they no longer think about going to the U.N. Security Council to try to settle the agruments that started the refugee affairs in the first place. They no longer think about going there until they have pushed hundreds of thousands of people outside their borders. That is a fairly grim notion. I mean it to be grim. I think it furnishes the backdrop of this whole discussion - a discussion which has referred to the application of general standards of behavior on the part of governments and of individuals to those who are helpless and the victims of the behaviors of those who made the earlier decisions.

With that introduction I ask members of the panel to volunteer to comment on each other's statements, to add to them or to refer to Bob DeVecchi's very good words.

Barry Stein: We leave off a word everytime we say 'refugees'. That word is 'political'. We should always be thinking that they are 'political refugees'. We can talk about the humanitarian aspects, but this is a very political area. Some said earlier that perhaps the limbo of the permanent camp is a somewhat new problem we're confronting. I would remind us all of the Palestinian refugees. After World War II, when the Palestinian problem appeared, a United Nations Relief and Works Agency was formed (UNRWA). One of the things we discovered is we don't want to try that solution ever again - one where you end up with permanent refugees. The danger may be that we are slipping into that with some of the new situations. The Palestinian example is a reminder of what we don't want to do.

Lionel Rosenblatt: I'd like to say something about the notion that the three classical approaches of voluntary repatriation, local settlement and resettlement in a third country are stretched awfully thin. My thought would be that we need to stretch each of these in a variety of directions, to cover the growth industry that unfortunately the refugee business has become. The refugee field is one of those areas which isn't going to go away, and the old traditional solutions are no longer adequate. I have not thought it through, but a temporary refuge along the lines perhaps of what the Australians have from time to time discussed, that is, something more than permanent limbo, but something less than full integration in the country of initial resettlement - in other words, a variation on either local settlement or resettlement - where, in the interim period the refugees are allowed to work and have some pride or self-sufficiency while the host country reaps some benefit and is not stuck permanently absorbing a new population might be a solution. And, as I suggested earlier, a temporary asylum near borders would also be beneficial.

One of the axioms, I gather, has been to move refugees away from borders because they are often insecure when they are near the borders. On the other hand, doing that loses an automatic, spontaneous voluntary repatriation capacity that, once they are moved away from the border, then has to be negotiated. Zia Risvi has suggested that negotiations are not going to succeed if the two governments have profound political differences between them.

Resettlement in a third country does not have to be in the U.S. and the other major countries of resettlement. France, Canada and Australia, in the case of the Indochinese, have taken more than their fair share. It hasn't just been the U.S. Proportionately, for example, New Zealand has accepted more Indochinese refugees than the U.S. That is something for people who feel we have done more than our fair share to remember.

I would suggest, though, that there are Belizes, which in the recent past have offered to resettle refugees. ICM and other organizations have a great potential role in figuring out how to make that kind of refugee resettlement cost-effective. I submit that if it is linked to development and other kinds of appeals to international financial institutions, governments can actually make a going concern of refugee resettlement. There is a whole province somewhere in the Amazon which is going belly-up in terms of not being able to attract enough people to work agriculturally on a new approach to paper harvesting and rice growing. Refugees could have contributed to keeping that kind of process alive. None of these resettlement plans are going to be easy. But, the disillusioning thing is that I see very little movement in any of these directions. Finally, early warning, an early dealing with the problem - an ounce of prevention - is far more important than anything we can do to expand the old solutions. I think that we have got to be much more vigilant about moving off the mark, at the first signs of the kind of things that we're seeing in Zimbabwe.

As a recent example, when Ruandans were coming out of Uganda it took months for governments and international organizations to make effective pleas. I am not talking about going through the motions, I am talking about effective leverage on Kampala. Nobody felt that it was their lead, nobody really followed through until 40,000 or 50,000 refugees had crossed. They are going to be a big ticket developed for the U.S. taxpayer, for the international taxpayer. That flow could have been modulated, dampened early on. The point is, the international mechanisms were not able to deal with either an early warning or an early response.

I don't know if this enters into the problem of the UNHCR not being able to get involved in 'root causes', and whether 'root causes' need to be addressed, therefore, by a combination of the private sector and any of these international agencies' lead governments. I think government working groups, with the most appropriately placed governments taking a lead to prevent refugee flows in a humane way, may be one way to explore. But, obviously, not only would we have to expand the existing solutions, but also prevent the problems from arising.

Robyn Ziebert: I would like to comment on the fact that one of the unique situations in Southeast Asia was in Hong Kong where the refugees were permitted to work. There were 70,000 at the height of the influx in '79 and early '80. There were 11 camps. A little over half of them were UNHCR camps, the others were run by Hong Kong prison authorities and the Immigration Service. They were open camps with the exception of one, which is where the refugees first came. All of the refugees of Hong Kong were permitted to work. They came and went as they pleased. It worked. It was a very good solution for Hong Kong. It filled the need, in terms of the economy of Hong Kong. They filled factory jobs, restaurant jobs, all sorts of things. But, what has happened is that Hong Kong itself feels that it has been saturated. They have since changed that law and Hong Kong camps are now closed camps. The people are no longer permitted to work. The Hong Kong government was afraid that this was a magnet which was attracting refugees. When the refugee processing centers were established in the Philippines and in Galang and in Indochina refugees from Thailand and Malaysia went happily. They got on their boats and in airplanes and they went to the RPCs. Refugees in Hong Kong fought tooth and nail; they did not want to be resettled in a refugee processing center where they might be for three months, or six months or a year. It didn't matter, you could promise them anything, but they were losing what they considered a measure of self-sufficiency and freedom. They didn't want to leave the large urban center where they had a measure of security and jobs. We had many problems in trying to convince them that they would have to go and that their resettlement would be affected a lot faster.

Bob DeVecchi: This has been far too polite. Let me be a little outrageous. Isn't there a political dimension that we are all avoiding in most of these discussions? Isn't there a political interest in the U.S. and the Western world to maintain the fiction that the Cambodian coalition along the border, fed by international food, aid and international money etc., is a viable alternative to the Vietnamese occupation of Cambodia? I might happen to agree with it, but isn't that the reality? Isn't part of the impetus of this behind the support for the UNHCR's appeal for funds to support three million Afghan refugees in Pakistan, based on keeping a viable force of muzhadin to fight the Soviet occupation? Similarly, don't such political ideas prevail in supporting the Eritrian liberation movements in the Sudan? Isn't it a bit hypocritical that the U.S., for example, deports El Salvadorian refugees who are asking nothing more than asylum, nothing more than a place to stay, nothing more than a bit of safety.

In this context, Hong Kong closed its borders over a year ago to refugees from the People's Republic of China. If a woman in Hong Kong gives birth to a child, and that person's husband manages to evade the sharks and swim across Deep Bay and land in Hong Kong, and then is picked up by the police, they are given only one alternative: the husband is sent back to China, and the mother and the child have to go too or they never see each other again. As a result the U.S., in its refugee admissions, has ceased to recognize that there is a possibility that there can be a political refugee from the largest Communist country in the world. Isn't there a political dimension to that?

Zia Risvi: I must say that I am not outraged. But if I were an American I would probably ask the same questions. I'll comment on one or two substantive points with regard to the solutions. I don't think the question really is to find a new solution or old solutions. The question is to find new approaches; methods to apply to the solutions which already exist. It is a problem of approach more than anything else. It amuses me and pains me sometimes that it is only when you have pain, that you know what pain is all about. Not when you have heard about it or read about it.

Indochina has been like that for America. When I heard the example about Kampucheans not being able to return, and not being able to resettle, and not being integrated in Thailand, I thought as though we were trying to re-invent the wheel and rediscover something that is there. The Burundi have been in Ruanda for many years. They cannot be repatriated, they have not been integrated, they cannot be resettled in the United States or Canada. Its not new but it's felt much more because the pain is here, because there is the problem of Kampucheans or Salvadorians or what have you.

There are two things that have occurred to me which are obvious. It should have been obvious to the international community for a long time, and yet it has not been addressed. One is what Lionel said earlier about early warning, which does not necessarily mean prevention, but could mean 'containment'. To a great extent it could also mean a 'preparedness'. There is no early warning system. The second thing is that the approach of the country of origin and the country of asylum must be simultaneous. There must be first of all a comprehensive view of the refugee situation: why are they leaving, how many are going to be leaving. Then, a bridge between the country of origin and the country of asylum which does not exist [must be built].

Even in the United Nations we take care of refugees in the country of asylum, and very often we don't go to the country of origin unless we feel there is a door which is open. An approach to a country of origin is political, not necessarily humanitarian. But beyond that, there are some very intrinsic problems that remain to be addressed in many situations - such as in the Third World, particularly Africa. Lionel talked about Ruanda and Uganda. What do you in a continent where countries have been created on the basis of artificial boundaries, and where tribal loyalty, is more important than national loyalty? Where the people who have gone from Uganda to Ruanda and those who came were the same people? They don't really know that they have crossed the border. Then people like me turn up and say, "Hey, man. You have become a refugee. I'm going to give you a paper and put you in a camp and you can stay there for twenty years. I am going to do good. I am going to bring you food." This is where the problem starts very often. Right now, in the case of Ruanda, there is a repatriation commission which is meeting again. The problem is not so much whether repatriation is possible or not, or whether it should be done or not - everybody agrees to that. They don't know who is Ruandan or who is a Ugandan to be repatriated to Uganda. In that type of problem, the solutions of this kind and generally good will would not help. Then what do you do? You don't address the refugee problem, you address the roots.

Again, in the case of roots there are words and acts. When I saw Sheppie Abramowitz in Thailand, she showed that one little good act was worth more than a thousand good words. Those countries which count, those countries which make a difference in global politics, have had their policies, their attitudes, determined essentially by either their internal politics or by their ideological inclinations. Somehow, after the Second World War, we learned that there were 'goodies and baddies', that the world was clearly divided. And whoever was on the bad side was a refugee who had to be helped when he came to the good side. Then suddenly we discovered that there was the whole big grey world of Africa and Asia.

One other matter which has not been addressed at all is a question of census; the question of numbers. Simply, how many refugees? I happen to come from Pakistan. Pakistan created a problem in 1971. At that time Pakistanis said, "We know the country, we know people living over there, we have gone through village by village and counted how many people have left." Therefore, officially the state said that two and ahalf million Pakistanis and Bengalis had left, had become refugees. The government of India at the same time said: "We have received the people in our country so that we know what we are talking about. We have counted them and they are ten million." Two and half million versus ten million.

We don't know how many refugees there really were. In fact, we don't even know what we are talking about in terms of numbers. And therefore, how do we plan aid projects? How do we multiply so many grains of rice by ten million, by two and a half million? And then, do we go into questions like the employment possibilities, the absorption capacity of the country of origin. People move out. Can the receiving country send them back? What are we going to do so that they can in fact absorb them and not make them refugees in their own country? This is a new phenomenon - the problem of returnees. What are the mechanisms that exist for protecting people once they are back home. For example, Ethiopia or Zaire were to come up with amnesty and people from Djihouti were to come back. Who is going to make sure that these people are not going to be cheated as far as amnesty is concerned. There is no mechanism: we could not go to the country of origin and say to the returnees we are going to protect you from your own government. The other part of it is assistance - is it possible that the donor can become more and more sensitive to helping the countries of origin; helping the "baddies", helping the people who created refugees, helping them in the first place so that they don't create refugees. That involves very critical thinking in the approach towards the problem and that does not exist.

Leon Gordenker: We must stop here. I thank the panel for a very informative session.

SELECTION AND ADMISSION

NORMAN Zucker: This panel is on "Selection and Admission". The previous panel was concerned with "Protection and Assistance". There is a difference. Protection and assistance basically deals with people who are not close to you. They are further away, so it is a matter of being less emotionally involved. But selection and admission hits closer to home. 'Selection and admission' - those are fancy words. They are lawyer words, professor words, they are INS words, State Department words. What selection and admission really means is "who gets in" and "why".

Historically our admission and asylum policies have not been particularly generous. I remember the remark of Mrs. Breckinridge. Many years ago, when Congress was debating whether or not to let in refugee children, someone said, "But they're little children. They're cute, they're little children." Her remark was: "Yes, but cute little children grow up to be ugly adults". There's this feeling of, "Well, we'll help them, but we won't help them come in". Because once in we're going to have to be bothered with these people.

Traditionally, we think of the Statue of Liberty, but that's only one side because traditionally we also have been nativistic; we have been xenophobic. God knows we certainly have been racist. There's a hostility to admission. Now we're seeing the same problems emerge. Aside from the very brief period after the Second World War when we were inundated with guilt and we changed our policy - just moderately - we now hear words that were tossed about this morning: Senator Simpson talking about "compassion fatigue" - that's a nice phrase- or "Refugee Inc." used by Senator Mazzoli. Unfortunately refugees are a growth industry. But, that's not the problem. The problem is how do we handle and make decisions regarding those whom we will admit. Can it comport with a humanistic and humanitarian posture *vis a vis* a policy which may well be parochial or subject to a very narrow definition of American national interest. Between these two we find we have contradictions and all sorts of inequities. When we have attitudes that say that we won't bring in Mrs. Allende - she was brought in by that well-known subversive group, some west coast Catholics - we have contradictions.

We will say to a twelve year old who says he gets a better bicycle in Chicago, we will give you asylum and you don't have to go home with your parents who want to take you home because you are going back to that bad land of Communist Russia. But, on the other hand, we'll take a busload of Salvadorans who are reasonably certain to be sent to death and ship them back across the border. We even go beyond that in that we have an active policy to cap refugee and migration flows. We interdict off Haiti, a policy which is legally dubious and certainly morally indefensible. More recently we've had Eliot Abrams make a statement that in El Salvador they are trying to put a cap on refugee migrations. These lead to all sorts of problems: of definitions, of understanding, of systemic conditions. To help sort out some of these problems we have three speakers this morning. David Pierce is "on loan" from the U.S. Foreign Service. He is now working with a consortium of cities in Orange County, helping to resettle and rectify some of the problems of resettlement. Prior to this he was in the Peace Corps. He went to work for the Foreign Service in 1973 and was posted to the Caribbean area. He'll tell us a little bit about the problems of definition, and to point out that admission and asylum policies are not that simple.

David Pierce: I find it very interesting that we have at this conference three people associated in one way or another with the Foreign Service, two of whom are still active Foreign Service officers. When I joined the Foreign service 10 years ago I was told in no uncertain terms, in my first few days in the service, that consular (read "immigration") work was not substantive foreign policy - that it was just processing people, the 'unwashed hordes', the same folks that we read about in Emma Lazarus' poem. It is no accident that those consular sections are usually in another part of the embassy, often in another part of town, because for a long time immigration has been regarded as not substantive foreign or economic policy. It was with some glee that I noted in the last few years that immigration and immigration kinds of issues - and I include refugee issues - have moved to the front of a lot of agendas. All you have to do is go down the list of countries that were mentioned in the last session, the list of regions that were mentioned and the scale of the flows of people across lines to recognize that we're looking at something, to use the double negative, that is not not substantive foreign policy. It is, in fact, one of the key elements of international relations and, I would even argue, international trade. Our whole sense of political and economic relationships, the models that we have to view the world, are tied up in it.

I speak as someone who has spent almost two years now working in Orange County, an area in California between Los Angeles and San Diego that has the highest concentrations of Indochinese refugees in the country, a county that has somewhere on the order of 10 percent of all the Indochinese in the U.S. in a population of 2 million or so - something close to seventy-some thousand Indochinese - and also quite a few 'undocumenteds' or unauthorized immigrants.

Here I'd like to take a look at definitional questions. The term 'displaced person', which is what used to be used to refer to refugees, has built within it the assumption of water displacement. When you put your hand in a bucket of water, the water is displaced. When that hand is removed, the water flows back to where it was. This is still what the term 'displaced person' means to many people: a temporary phenomenon brought on by an intervention of some strange, unusual, unplanned, unexpected, inappropriate event. When that intervention is stopped or removed, when that force moves away, things flow back to where they were.

We don't generally think of it as a full bucket in which a hand is put in and things spill over the side, and they don't go back by themselves. Yet that is really what we mean in most cases and what the general public means when they think of refugees. Although we have talked about repatriation as one of the solutions, or one of the possible steps to resolve the problem, the fact is that the term refugee has come to mean not temporary displacement but some permanent status. These are folks who are going to be gone from where they came from for a long time, maybe for their whole lives. That is an important distinction.

Why I raise this is because within the term 'refugee' we have long term folks. We have another term for asylum. "Asylum" is like "displaced persons". It is a temporary haven until the 'smoke blows over', until a 'hand' is removed from the 'bucket'.

We don't always make those distinctions clear in our discussions. When we talk about refugees as a general category, we sometimes lose the distinctions between temporary and permanent. Also implicit in the words and the concepts are the questions of motivations - not only where are they going and when, but why they are out of their country of origin - why they left.

We tend to assume in our thinking that even the phrase 'political migrant' or 'economic migrant' assumes two different sets of motivations, and that they are easy to distinguish. My own feeling is that they are not easy to distinguish. They tend to break down in a situation where resources are so scarce, or politics are so oppressive or confiscatory, that the situations arise where folks feel, whether accurately or not, that they face death either for themselves or for their children, or face some equally difficult future. At that point, are they economic migrants or political migrants?

If it is the political forces in the country that are so arrayed that large numbers of people are increasingly unable to meet basic survival needs, or basic needs with dignity, are they political migrants, are they leaving for political reasons or for economic reasons? The proximate cause may be economic, "Well they don't have enough calories, they don't have enough food", but in fact the ulimate source may be the political structure. In fact, if this sounds a little familiar to some of the debates over refugees and migrants, that question is at the heart of one. I admit that this is not an easy question to deal with.

Let me give you an example from my own experience with small island countries, the mini-states of the Caribbean - for example, Antigua. When I was a desk officer, many years ago, Antigua had an economy that had roughly half of its working age population in the United States in one variety of status or another, or outside of Antigua in some metropole. Of those who remained, approximately a third were employed by the government and a third in the private sector. Politics in the country centered on who, what group, what political grouping was going to get those government jobs. And, when the politics changed, virtually every job in the public sector changed hands.

While I am exaggerating to make the point, in effect the one-third that was unemployed and that remained in the country took those public sector jobs that were vacated by the third that had been pushed out by the political change. Now, fortunately, many of those who lost their jobs had a cushion from the many who were sending remittances. But, if someone chose to leave after an election in which they were forced out of the only possible means of livelihood they could have in the country - remember we're dealing with extremely limited resources - is that person's motivation 'political' or 'economic'? That is not an easy question. The point is that we have not been able, either in our laws or in our practice, to make those fine distinctions very well.

Part of the reason we haven't been able to make those distinctions has to do with the nature of political analysis of international relations and also of economic relations, particularly trade and finance.

The fundamental, unstated assumption, in both political and economic analyses, is that 'borders' mean something; that 'lines' mean something; that people don't move over them normally; that it is an exception, an emergency; it is a war; it is an unusual event; it is persecution by government; it is any number of things and it is a specific knowable cause. Our analyses tend in both of these areas to see flows of people across these lines we have erected in our minds, on our maps, and by treaties and everything else, as unusual; not the norm, but the exception.

I have just spent more than a year and a half living in southern California, within a hundred miles of the 'official' border with Mexico. I defy anybody to tell me exactly where the border, *de facto,* is. Certainly the Mexican territory includes large parts of the city of Santa Ana, large parts of the city of Los Angeles, probably large parts of the Imperial Valley. What we see on a map, the concept, the "model" we have in our head of this nice clean beautiful line arrived at by military actions, by treaties and so on, does not necessarily match the territory. Reality is quite different in many cases and in many places and in many times. What does it do to our concept of national interest, or economic trade, or any of those concepts on which our views of the world are built when we recognize that this country has large populations from other nation-states - working age populations - that live in the areas where they are clearly identified by where they came from?

Another area that we have already talked about this morning is the 'overlap' between political and economic motivations. The so-called 'magnet' effect that was implicitly referred to in connection with Hong Kong was the basis of the Thai action, as I understand it, in making camps in Thailand austere - so as to reduce the attractiveness of that. Now, is that 'political' or 'economic'? The assumption is it's an 'economic' magnet, an economic motivation.

Considering the distinction between 'stock' and 'flow', many of the solutions that are proposed or tried for dealing with the stock of people who have already come here, that are already among us and are part of us, affect the flow. Often we don't distinguish that. One of the first things that the Carter Administration did was to determine that it was not humane to try to lock up all the Haitians they knew of in South Florida. They began issuing temporary work permits. That was a humane response. We didn't have the space nor the money to buy the space in jails anyway. The humane response was to temporarily allow the Haitians to work while we were going through the long drawn-out process of individual review of asylum applications under the law in effect at that time. If that was the only question, one could argue that it was a very humane response - humanitarian and humane. But, it is argued, the result of such a response would be a 'magnet effect', a stimulator to the flow. And the numbers of Haitians leaving both Haiti and the Bahamas did increase. Some of those Haitians got to the U.S., and some of them died at sea. Now, if someone knew in advance the way to deal with the stock was humanitarian, to provide work permits for 1,000 Haitians, let's say, and if one knew that, for every hundred Haitians who are in this stock of those receiving work permits - over the course of a year - five other Haitians from either Haiti or the Bahamas would die in the attempt to join the stock, how would one balance humanitarian objectives? Presumably you don't want to do anything that will encourage folks to risk their lives, whether it is for political or economic reasons.

Let me touch on the balance question of "how many can we take?" We had the suggestion that we have an active policy to cap overflows. In numerical terms, I would go back to the Statue of Liberty. Many of us don't remember that four years before the Statue of Liberty was dedicated in 1886, we passed the first of our 'exclusion acts'. The Chinese Exclusion Act began a series of restrictions on racial and ethnic grounds that only ended in law with the 1965 act. Even while the Statue of Liberty was being built we had already had this dichotomy of controlling, of borders that we thought were ours to control with the idea of being a nation of immigrants, a country that had done very well be being a nation of receiving immigrants.

There are problems of absorptive capacity: How many people can we take in a community? Often the question is not financial, though that is part of it. Often the question is social: How many people can we take, how fast, in a community before the social fabric begins to unravel? And it is not always a racist or racial question. If you put 77,000 Swedes into downtown Orange County in the space of three years you would have problems until those Swedes, who have blue eyes and blonde hair and so on, began to speak and behave the same way as everybody else.

The second problem is the stability of nations overseas. Stability not in the sense of 'status-quo-no-change', but predictability; no massive sudden shifts. That's the kind of stability - both domestic and foreign - we're looking for. Often there is a trade-off. How many can we take here before the situation becomes unraveled at home and we get vigilante action, or we get community hostility, or we get shootings and violence, or we get fights in the schools? How many can we take and match that against how many we must take, ourselves and others, to keep the situation stable in other parts of the world, so that the same thing doesn't happen there? This is a whole other kind of trade-off.

Let me see if that raises a question. I simply want to suggest one other thing; while we talk about an active policy to cap inflows, the fact is that the U.S. has one of the most open immigration policies in the world. Not on paper, not in the law, but *de facto*. And that has to do with the 1952 law. We have, in fact, absorbed large numbers of people under the table, underground railroad, whatever you want to call it - and, we continue to do so. In addition to the 800,000 people we took in 1930, officially, we may well have taken an equal number or more net, without official sanction, so that in fact we have a fairly good track record of absorbing a lot of people.

Norman Zucker: Thank you very much. I would like to exercise the prerogative of the chair and make three comments.

When we deal with asylum we must never forget that we are dealing with people. And when we talk about assumptions of permanence, it behooves us to remember Keynes' dictum, that in the long run, they're all dead. The second point is that when David was talking about the humane response on the part of the administration, I would like to remind this audience that part of the humane response came about because there was a nudge by two people on this panel who were instrumental in bringing forth Judge King's decision in the Haitian case. Thirdly, when you mentioned absorptive capacity I was reminded of a story of Chaim Weizmann when he was testifying before one of the innumerable British Royal commissions. They had just presented him with a huge expert's report that Palestine could not take a single new immigrant. The absorptive capacity of the land was surfeited. Weizmann's comment was "Gentlemen, each immigrant and refugee who enters the land, brings with him his own absorptive capacity in his suitcase". I think we forget refugees bring benefits.

David Pierce: My personal feeling is that we have always benefited in economic terms, in terms of human capital, in terms of social and other contributions. My observation about 'absorptive capacity' has to do with political limits, it has to do with social cohesion and it really is a 'future shock'. It's an Alvin Toffler kind of concept. It is: How flexible is the community? How flexible can it be made in absorbing folks with different behavior patterns and in tolerating that? I don't see it as an economic problem at all. If I had to argue I would argue that it is by far and clearly an economic benefit almost everywhere and almost at all times. It's the social cohesion and how far can you go before the thing starts to come unglued. That is the question and it is fundamentally a political question; not a resource question.

Norman Zucker: Okay. We'll hold that. I'd like to introduce now Michael Posner. He is currently Executive Director for the Lawyers Committee for Human Rights. He grew up in Chicago, went to Berkeley and became a lawyer. He turns up like a good penny, whenever you can find him testifying before Congress, giving testimony before courts on behalf of what some people might call "the good guys".

Michael Posner: I want to brief and make four or five relatively simple points in an obviously complicated area. From the previous presentations, from Dale DeHaan's comments, from some things that David Pierce has said, it is clear that this is not a simple problem. Nonetheless, there are a few simple comments that may be made to help direct the discussion of our admission and selection process.

First, I disagree with one thing David Pierce says. I think the law that we have in place today governing refugees and asylum is basically a law that is workable. The words of the law provide a framework for both regular refugee admissions and determination of asylum claims. It is based on the principles of the U.N. convention relating to the status of refugees, now a 30 year old document. It was a painful process, as Dale DeHaan well knows, that got us to pass the Refugee Act in 1980, and at least it sets the framework for an intelligent policy. What we need now is to figure out a way to implement it efficiently, economically and fairly. It is to that issue I want to address my remarks.

First, I think we are burdened by history. It is an history, as we have heard this morning, that is humanitarian with regard to treatment of Eastern Europeans, Indochinese, Cubans, where substantial numbers of people have been resettled in this country; people fleeing persecution. It is also a tradition that has always been limited, and limited in terms of an ideological bias. There are blinders on our policy. The blinders are reflected clearly in the words of the McCarren-Walter Act, the governing immigration statute in this country on the subject of refugees from 1952 until 1980. It defined a refugee as somebody coming from a Communist, or Communist-dominated country, who has a well-founded fear of persecution. I would submit that this theory and ideological and geographical mind-set or viewpoint still dominates the system almost exclusively. One year after, the U.N. Convention Relating to the Status of Refugees was passed because the U.N. Convention adopted a very different approach. It talked about refugees as being people with a well-founded fear of persecution - persecution based on race, religion, nationality, membership in a social class, or political opinion. It didn't talk about ideology. It didn't have a geographical preference - at least on paper. The definition stands as a universal statement. It was finally incorporated in our law with the passage of the Refugee Act of 1980. I think that is a good place for us now to begin to work to make it a law that has meaning and has equitable treatment for all people.

The second concern is economic. The refugees are now subsumed into a broader debate about how many foreign people we can tolerate in our country. It is an economic issue. It is also a question of national character and identity. There are certainly racial and other prejudices involved that we can't run away from. Nonetheless, I think it is important to view the refugee aspect of migration as a separate category - that isn't to say totally separable, but one that has always been treated slightly or somewhat differently than normal migration for a variety of reasons: personal, family ties, economic, etc.

It is certainly true, as David has pointed out, and this raises a third point, that the definition of who is a refugee is a difficult business. I quite agree that when one looks to most individuals who are either applying for refugee admission overseas or come here and seek asylum, it is generally the case that [their motives] are not purely political, economic or personal: generally all sorts of factors are at play. The difficult decisionmaking that needs to be done is to sort out those factors. I personally view the refugee definition contained in the Convention, and now in our law, as a sensible starting place. It is, in some respects, limited. There is now some pressure, for example, to broaden it in cases where there is civil strife, such as a country like El Salvador. There is pressure from some quarters to broaden it so that every Haitian would be considered a refugee from the general malaise that afflicts that country. In countries that suffer under dictatorial regimes where people are persecuted, the persecution doesn't take the same forms. Thus, for example, a Haitian security force member with unclear ties to the government may be involved in a personal incident with somebody. There are very few political leaders in Haiti because there are no political parties. There are very few labor leaders because the labor unions have been barred. There are very few student leaders because it is simply not permitted. Most independent journalists have been kicked out of the country. It's not the sort of situation that lends itself to a classic definition of a refugee. These are difficult problems to be sure, but I think we have to confront them fairly and we have to confront them in a similar way - whether we are dealing with Indochinese, Haitians, Salvadorans or Soviet Jews.

The next factor, and the one that I deal with most regularly in my business, is an administrative, bureaucratic concern of how we implement the law at home and abroad. Let's take abroad first.

We now have a refugee act that allows a certain amount of refugee admissions every year. It is down from a figure of well over 200,000 in the later 1970s to just over 80,000 for this year. Latin America is entitled to only 3,000 slots. In fact, for fiscal year 1982, the last year in which we have statistics, of the 3,000 slots for Latin America, only 579 refugees were admitted into the U.S. It is an incredible figure given the chaos occurring throughout our hemisphere. Of the 579 refugees, 577 were from Cuba. There were two refugees through regular admissions programs and both were from Argentina. That is a remarkable figure, but it is not unusual.

It reflects the pattern of the last three years since the refugee act has been created. The statistics, when you come to domestic asylum applications - that is, people who have arrived in the U.S. either under another status as student or visitor and sought asylum, or more typically, have come illegally, without documents, and sought asylum once they're arrived (Salvadorans, Haitians are classic examples) - are striking. Of more than 5,000 Haitian asylum applications pending in 1982, three were granted asylum. The numbers for other countries: four from the Philippines; three from Pakistan; none from Chile; none from Guatemala. The fact is that we have a refugee policy and an aslyum policy still based on the McCarren-Walter Act definition of who a refugee is. It reflects itself administratively in a lack of any sort of institutional effort by the State Department, by the Immigration Service, and I suppose by the UNHCR and voluntary agencies as well to set up permanent, effective and broad-reaching admissions programs for Latin America, Africa, or Asia outside of Indochina. There simply isn't the apparatus, there isn't the discussion, there aren't the experts that we hear today talking about Indochina who know and are able to work bringing people from, say, Guatemala, El Salvador and Haiti to the U.S.

There are reasons for this. That leads me to a fifth point which is that this is a very political system. The greatest work that still needs to be done is to try to bring back the humanitarian ideals that characterized our policy with regard to the Europeans who came after the war, and with regard to the Indochinese - a policy that is fair, that is even-handed, and that deals with people on the basis of need, on the basis of the severity of their persecution. The fact that zero Salvadorans have been granted refugee status in the last three years is a national disgrace. We can say that they're being put into Honduras, that they are being sent here and there. The fact is that we have a responsibility to take part of that burden. If we don't take it through a regular admission process, people are going to come anyway, as we have seen and as we now know well, and we're going to have a crisis that is greater than we face today.

I am not suggesting that these are easy problems to solve. What I am saying is, in an area where there are limited resources, where people are reluctant to accept more foreigners, more non-English speakers, more drain to our already over-crowded employment lines, we have to be careful to select people who have clear claims for persecution, people who are clearly refugees, and do it in as humane a way as possible, being as fair as possible.

One final comment, in regard to the Immigration Service handling of asylum cases in the U.S. - I could go on at length about that but I won't - it is a bureaucracy probably without parallel in the U.S. federal system that is mismanaged and indifferent to a very serious problem.

There is no effort, very little effort, that I have seen in five years working on this problem to respond in a humane and caring way to the genuine problems of people seeking political asylum in this country. It is viewed politically, it is viewed as something that ought to be decided by the State Department. It is viewed as an extension of our foreign policy and it is essentially viewed by the Immigration Service as another pain, another drain on resources, and another impediment to their enforcement capability.

I suggest that there needs to be better training, better supervision, greater input in that process by UNHCR and other experts in the field, and greater humanity - a greater sense of the dimensions of the problem. I suggest, in that regard, that there is a great deal of ink wasted, a great deal of discussion in the halls of Congress about massive flows of people of mass asylum. I suggest that we take the problem and look at it from another perspective - that is, the individual applicant from the faraway place, let's say the Philippines, or Pakistan, or South Korea, coming to this country and applying for asylum.

Nobody is thinking about how to treat individual cases - we're confronted with massive numbers and we tend to become paralyzed in our discussion of how we're going to deal with 50,000 Salvadorans, or 1,700 Haitians. In fact, if you look at the statistics the Immigration Service cites, there is something in the neighborhood of 130,000 pending claims for political asylum. That is a slightly misleading figure, misleading in part because they never seem to resolve any of the cases, and there are something in the neighborhood of 55,000 Cuban cases that sit idling with nobody paying any attention. If you look at the figures for 1982, there were 33,000 claims for political asylum. Now, if you deduct the figure for four countries - El Salvador, Nicaragua, Iran and Poland - there are only 8,000. So, we're not dealing with a problem that is quite as unmanageable as is portrayed. In fact we only granted 3,400 people in the country political asylum last year. These are not striking numbers. In Orange County there are probably tens of thousands of people coming this month, illegally, who are never going to be detected. We're not dealing with a massive number of people coming to this country, but really with a very few who are seeking political asylum through this process. We can resolve the problem if there is the institutional will to do so. But it is primarily a question of that will being generated from the public and from the members of Congress who will implement and oversee a badly fated immigration and State Department implementation process.

Norman Zucker: Mike's last comments touched on the problem of asylum and it leads into the differences between the group definitions of asylum and individual cases. In his comments regarding State Department bureaucracy, he mentioned 130,000. The last time I checked they had two full-time people and one half-time person dealing with nearly 130,000 asylum claims, which indicates the Department's view of the urgency of the situation.

One group which gets the government to move is the lawyers. We have several with us. One is Dale Frederick Swartz, who to some extent is returning home. He went to Amherst. He then went to the University of Chicago and then went to work for a major Washington law firm. He headed up the Alien Rights Law Group for a while and he was of counsel in the landmark *Haitian Refugee Center v. Civiletti.* Now Rick is Executive Director of the National Immigration, Refugee and Citizen Forum, which is working to bring about a coherent, comprehensive, and I hope humane refugee policy.

Rick Swartz: Thank you. What I am going to try to to do is just simply comment on some of the main themes that David and Mike presented to you. I'm not going to try to come up with a coherent organization to my comments, but almost seriatum go through their major points and perhaps provide a little bit of elaboration, and then talk about a couple of things that Norman suggested.

David began with a theme that immigration heretofore has not been seen as a foreign policy issue. It has not been part of the systematic apparatus of the State Department, the National Security Council, other agencies in the government and private sector concerned with international relations and foreign policy. I think most of us agree that has ceratinly been the case. He also suggested that he thinks that is changing. Now I think that it probably is changing, but boy, is it slow. Very slow. One of the challenges to those concerned with these questions is whether or not foreign policy - international relations - is an integral part of the migration debate (I think it is but others disagree) and if it is, does there need to be political organizing and hard core public education to try to shift the focus of the debate about immigration and refugee policies away from the issue of domestic impact? The national and public debate today, as I observe it in Washington, is domestic impact; domestic concern. It may not be serving the national interest in the long term or the short term. I think it is a very important issue for the academic community, for the activist community, for the operational community and needs more attention from all of us.

David also talked about definitions and labels, and I certainly agree that it is important. It is important not only because there are legal implications to concepts and words that are used in this field. Refugee is now part of our law. The concept of 'asylee' is now in the law. What does it mean, legally? What does it mean in application? What does it mean to the decision makers? What does it mean to members of Congress who think about it five or ten minutes a year as opposed to those more intimately involved in this process? What does it mean to the public at large? My observation, and I think that many of you would share this, is that these labels and these words and these concepts and what they mean in terms of human beings are all being mixed up together. Sharp distinctions are not being drawn when it comes down to the politics of these issues. I am going to give you one quick example that I talk about to the refugee community.

There is now, as you know, a major legislation being debated in Congress called the Simpson-Mazzoli Bill. It does deal with political asylum, but its major focus is undocumented or illegal immigration, legal immigration and the treatment of the undocumented now in this country. Another major issue that is being presented is that of temporary foreign workers - guest workers, "H2" workers, as they are known in the bill. I called my office and got a quick report on a debate, on a hearing yesterday. The agricultural interest in the U.S., who want to have changes in the law so they can have greater flexibility to bring in temporary foreign workers, are throwing around figures for the first time publicly. Two to three hundred thousand temporary foreign workers a year are coming in under a legal program. Now, to the public and to most of the decisionmakers, refugees and illegal aliens and legal immigrants and two to three hundred thousand guest workers are all one and the same. They are people coming in, especially to the public at large. I think the refugee community has a very strong and immediate interest in this debate over guest workers and "H2" because, if this law is changed and in two years from now 300,000 guest workers are coming in, there is going be a lot more pressure to keep refugee numbers down. There will be more concern at the state and local government level because these guest workers are going to need health care and other things. It's going to cost money and the easiest flow to turn off is that flow from Indochina, and the flow from Afghanistan - the people who are far away as opposed to Haitians, Salvadorans and Mexicans. Refugee-concerned people should be very involved in the debate over guest workers and I don't see enough evidence of that happening.

David talked about motivations, as did Michael, and the difference and the difficulty of discerning between economic and political. I don't think much more needs be said about that except to remind you what the law is, because the Refugee Act of 1980 and the U.N. Protocol and even the Reagan Administration's interpretation of it make clear that the determinative legal question is not why people left their homelands, but whether they have a well-founded fear of persecution upon return. That was the heart of the debate in the Haitian litigation that we did. In many respects nobody was claiming that every single Haitian was persecuted in Haiti and that was the reason why they took to the seas. But we thought we proved conclusively, and certainly to the satisfaction of a federal judge after a seven week trial, that at that time, 1979-80, the Haitian government had a policy that those returned were spies and traitors to be sought out and destroyed.

As long as that policy was in effect, even if only three out of ten might become the victims, virtually every Haitian had a "well-founded fear of persecution" because it was so arbitrary.

That reminded me of a point that was made in the earlier panel: Do we give refugee-asylum applicants the benefits of doubt? Again, in the Haitian context or the Salvadoran context, some would argue the benefit of the doubt is the U.N. protocol, or at least the handbook on the protocol indicates it should be given to asylum applicants, and an awful lot of folks, legally, are going to qualify. Remember, though, what the legal definition is. Then that comes back to the politics.

There has been, for the last year or year and a half, much more interest in some sectors of Congress in re-examining refugee policy and the

Refugee Act in these legal norms precisely with an eye towards changing that definition so that we would in fact abandon or step away from the protocol and adopt as a matter of statutory law a definition that to be termed an asylee or a refugee, you have the burden of proving persecution as the cause for fleeing. If you can't do it, life is hard. Even if you'd be persecuted upon return, we're going to send you back because the law will have been modified. That is something to watch this year in Congress.

David talked about assumptions, about borders and the concept of sovereignty. Again, that is an important point. There are some philosophers and academics in this country who are doing some interesting thinking, re-examining the concept of sovereignty, the concept of borders, and the context of the flow and migration of people.

One of the reasons I believe that there has been such resistance to Haitians, Salvadorans, Guatemalans and others in this hemisphere being recognized by the U.S. government as refugees is because they are so close to us. A number of other considerations include ideology, the relations of those countries, backlash and the politics in local communities impacted. When I was doing the Haitian work day in and day out the concept of "magnet effect" kept coming up. If we acknowledge Salvadorans as refugees then it's going to increase the magnet effect. Look at the situation in Southeast Asia where everybody is a refugee, creating greater incentives for those to try to make themselves refugees by the act of fleeing. The proximity to the U.S. of refugees or would-be refugees in this hemisphere is having a big impact on the thinking of those in the U.S. government who are concerned about the flood-gates opening up.

In reference to the comments in the earlier panel about the change of the practices in Hong Kong of releasing refugees from the camps into the community, this is an example of the linkage between immigration policy and refugee policy. At hearings recently on the question of employer sanctions - that is, making it unlawful for employers to hire undocumented aliens, a centerpiece of efforts now to control illegal immigration - the Attorney General, in response to questions that if sanctions haven't worked any place else, so the GAO reports, why are we looking at sanctions here, he said, "Well I've just been in Hong Kong and in Hong Kong they are enforcing employer sanctions and it's working". I'd be interested in talking with those of you who know something about the Hong Kong experience to see if that's true, or what the trigger for this greater enforcement of sanctions has been. I presume it might have some relation to the changes and practices of allowing refugees to live in camps and work in the community. But, there are linkages there, and refugees, communities and Americans working with them have to pay attention to immigration policy and the politics that surround it because that is the way decisions are being made.

Balance - how many can we take. David talked about this: short term and long term views. Sure our unemployment is 10.4 percent and that is discussed all the time in this country especially concerning immigration and refugee issues. The Rand Corporation, however, and some demographers have recently issued reports which project that in 15 to 20 years this country is going to be labor poor. That is, that given low fertility rates and projections about the changing character of our economy, including moving into a service economy, we're going to need workers in the relatively near future, that are "domestic stock", that citizens and immigrants now here simply are not going to provide because of birth rates. If there is some truth to that projection, should that not be a central part of the debate today about immigration and refugee policies? Can we take a bit more of a long-term view? The political answer is no, because the politics around this question don't allow those politicans so inclined to think long-term. Again, one of the challenges before us is, how can we be realistic about politics and advocacy and political action so that some decision makers feel it is a bit more safe to be courageous and a bit more safe to say to the U.S. public: "Even if it's tough now, it's within our national interest to make decisions today with an eye to 20 years, or 30 years or 40 years from now". It is very hard for politicians to do this without feeling that they are taking great risks by going against that 90 percent who think we've got enough people in this country already.

Michael says the law is workable, it's a good framework. I tend to agree, but I'll point to Bryan Walsh, who reminds us that the 1980 Refugee Act has not addressed, in a legal clearcut way, the mass first asylum phenomena. There are some things in the law which could have and should have been used in 1980, like the Emergency Powers provision of the act. A fair question might be: Is there a framework that exists today to deal adequately with Haitians, Salvadorans, Guatemalans, significant numbers of people coming to our shore and seeking asylum. It is hard to do individual determinations in a fair way when the numbers are significant.

That brings me back to another comment of Mike's - that is the ideological bias and practice as opposed to what the law says. There can be no doubt about it. I read a paper produced by the Refugee Policy Group which made an interesting point: the tradition of asylum through the ages has been that the granting of asylum or refugee status is not to be interpreted as an action of aggression against the country from which people have fled. Yet, asylum is being used or seen or perceived as an act of aggression by many today. Maybe that is why we're not granting asylum to Haitians or Salvadorans who clearly have a well-founded fear, while we do so with regard to those from the Soviet Union. We're using it with regard to Southeast Asia with regard to ideological purposes.

Statistics on asylum- my last comment on Michael's remarks, and then just a few other thoughts. He is absolutely right. His one hundred ten, one hundred twenty, one hundred thirty thousand figure is flying around Washington all the time. It's stretching the truth a bit. It is not being challenged effectively either. All of us are letting that go on. Nobody is saying to Simpson or Mazzoli: "Excuse me sir, but you're not telling the truth on this".

One reason is because there has been a lot of political pressure coming out of Florida over the last couple of years. There's a broader reason: the

Reagan administration is very anxious to get the courts out of this business so that we can't bring Haitian Refugee Center lawsuits again in the future. The statistics become a significant part of the debate or the so-called rationale for sweeping changes in the asylum laws that are now under consideration. I don't think the government officials know exactly what they're doing. It's part of their political strategy and [we] should think about what an appropriate response might be.

Finally, a couple of thoughts on Norman's themes. When I was at Amherst, I wrote a thesis, the title of which was: "The Limits of Cultural Pluralism". I didn't know I was going to get into this Immigration/Refugee issue quite the way I have. I looked at public schools in New York City in the late 1800s when the schools were being used to Americanize and acculturate. The progressive reformers, as I analyzed the situation, wanted to centralize the programs, in part to get the patronage away from the Irish and in part to more effectively use the schools to Americanize newcomers about whom they were concerned because they were different. I still think that the cultural pluralism question here is a very important one.

I believe in politics and in organizing - on the local level, on the national level. Most members of Congress who have voted on these issues are making their decisions by the size of the stack of mail they get. Don't kid yourselves about it. There are no more than 10 members of the House of Representatives, in my judgment, who have a significant education about these issues. The rest of them are voting because they are going to follow Rodino, they are going to follow Mazzoli, they are going to follow Democratic leadership, or they are going to look at the size of the mail from their constituents. The mail coming from those who think we've got enough people here - refugees, immigrants, whatever - is high, and the mail from those thinking maybe it is in our self-interest to take a somewhat longer-term view, that stack is small.

David Pierce: One of the key distinctions we have to keep in mind that I didn't stress was the difference between *de facto* and *de jure*. On the books, we have a restrictive immigration law, we have a restrictive asylum policy. In fact, if we have anything like half a million Salvadorans in the country we have a wide open asylum policy, de facto not de jure, and we have the world's largest temporary worker program, already well over a million people. I don't think anyone would challenge that we have at least a million new arrivals of temporary workers every year, although they don't all stay. To take one of his points, we need to recognize that we don't have a closed door, but we do have dichotomies and double standards between what the law says and what in fact is. As the Simpson-Mazzoli and similar kinds of things move forward, the fundamental attempt being made is to redress that dichotomy - between de facto and de jure. We need to look at whether that is possible, and whether that is desirable; whether we really do want to restrict immigration, or whether we want to pull out some of the stuff that is now de facto and put it up where it is de jure, and how best to do that.

RESETTLEMENT

GRETCHEN Brainerd: I am the Washington representative of the Intergovernmental Committee for Migration, ICM, which was mentioned by several panelists this morning.

Resettlement comes, appropriately, at this point in our discussions. It is that third option of what you do when you're faced with movement of people out of their countries. The first, you will remember, is to repatriate them after the situation in their country is improved; the second, settlement in place [local integration]; third is third country resettlement. Now we're talking about the third country option and particularly what happens in the U.S.

We have on this panel people who are resettlement coordinators or who are in charge of resettlement policy for voluntary agencies in different parts of the U.S. We are going to start off with Michael Friedline, the Regional Coordinator for World Relief, a voluntary agency sponsored by the National Association of Evangelicals. His home base is in Orange County, California. He is also currently the chair of the Los Angeles Refugee Forum. He's going to talk about the California perspective on refugee resettlement.

Michael Friedline: I was pleased to be asked to come and present a view from the trenches. Sometimes we feel that it is a legionnaires outpost that has been forgotten.

Many of the resettlement problems today are centered in California simply because most major resettlement our country has done has been with the Indochinese and a great majority of them have either been resettled initially in, or have moved to California. Right now it is estimated that about one third of all the refugees resettled in the U.S. reside in California - not just Indochinese but all ethnic groups, so there is a certain validity to what maybe has been characterized as a "California perspective".

I see a divergence between some basic assumptions about resettlement and the policies that grow out of some of these assumptions. Failure to see resettlement as it has become for the majority of the refugees inhibits the development of effective policy and response to issues. Too often we mistakenly blame the refugees for not fitting into, or prospering according to a traditional model we have developed, when we in fact the model, or maybe numerous models, are not addressing the real problems themselves.

Let me present a practical example. Traditionally, resettlement was seen as a one-on-one proposition. An individual or a group, perhaps a church, perhaps some caring people in the community, decided to get involved with refugees. They were usually established people, native born Americans, or those who emigrated and became firmly adapted to our society. They brought with them opportunities to get involved, warm hearts and lots of resources. They accepted the new persons and their families from "over there", from wherever "there" might be, and took them from a point of total dependence, right off the track or plane, to a point of successful independence. In other words, they saw them through all the immediate needs and stayed with them until they became adjusted, understood life in the U.S. and were successfully working and on their way to building new lives. This, of course, meant that the persons involved in this process were pretty much the 'stars' of the show. They were the ones who were needed and they, in turn, had the opportunity to make many good things happen. There was a good deal of re-inforcement given to them. They got to see the process from the beginning to completion.

In resettlement programs that brought in a small number of people on a regular basis, especially those with people coming from cultures that had already established themselves in the U.S., ...[this] was a largely workable model. What changed with the Indochinese influx was that there were large numbers of people coming all at once with great needs and no strongly established ethnic community. They couldn't be accomodated with models that were utilized before. More voluntary agencies were added in the years between 1975-1980 to help bring out the resources of the private sector. More programs were started. But, we were forced to change from the highly personal model to somewhat of a mass production model of resettlement. It was necessary. It has its advantages and disadvantages.

In the alternative example a refugee is sponsored by a voluntary agency, perhaps with the help of a relative who preceded home to this country not long before, and is receiving assistance of some sort and still trying to pull himself up to a point of security and independence. The relative (if there is one) has few resources to give, but he does have the ability to show the newcomer how to use the services that are available in the area. He takes care of such things as the health screening, helps with Social Security, registration for welfare, getting into English programs, or job programs. The relative can also do one other valuable thing - he can tell the newcomer how it really is here. It becomes an orientation and it is based on fact rather than on a vision of what we would like the fact to be. In other words, it is truly orientation and not indoctrination. The strength of that, of course, is that the refugee has a very clear idea in a very short time as to what the situation is; he is hearing it from someone he trusts.

The voluntary agency case workers usually take care of crises and emergencies and spend little time with each family. Refugees do not learn all about the U.S. in one session, or when they see a movie, or when they see it on a blackboard and get all the answers explained. It is an ongoing process. The advantage of having a guide who is with them throughout the process is that whenever they have a question they can ask it. However, when a case worker checks in with them only periodically, they might not have a question at the time of the visit, but later they may have a need and there is no one readily available to help. They have to call, or make an appointment and go down to the office. With rising numbers and increasing pressures, you end up relying on the less personal model.

We've responded to new needs by creating a mass production system where voluntary agencies, social service projects, county agencies, welfare programs and community groups all play a part in the resettlement of the refugees. We're all bit-part players. We lose our 'stardom' in a sense and become cogs in a line. If we all worked well together the product would come out all right, but there are many apparent weaknesses. Some have to do with rivalries and overlapping responsibilites. All are related to making the more complex system work. For instance, a problem for a voluntary agency is that while we can take care of initial needs, we must then refer the refugee to others, like an ESL [English as a Second Language] program. Sometimes the ESL program isn't as good as we had hoped it would be. Or perhaps the refugee has to stay longer and does not move towards self-sufficiency. Or we refer a person to a job agency that is overloaded and can't get the refugee a job. All of a sudden the system breaks down. To counter this, in many places in the western U.S. we have developed consortiums or forums. A forum is basically a loose knit group of service providers from all elements and different types of funding agencies that gather together for four major reasons. First, they reinforce the relationships between those people working in agencies. If you know someone, you can call him or her up; if you don't, you have to go through a lot of red tape to accomplish anything. The second reason that forums exist is to share information. This is a field where, as we all know, many things happen very quickly. Forums are able to be on top of legislation, on top of community problems, and by sharing information we can stay on the same track. A third reason for having forums is to organize advocacy programs. Refugees, especially the Indochinese, have no political power base, at least not yet. Many have not become citizens and have not yet been politically socialized to American ways. They are generally unable to effectively impact on the political system despite the fact that they are often concentrated in given areas. They need advocates. We, as service providers with some sort of a sense of 'mission' in helping the refugees, often become the spokespersons for the refugees in our communities and with state and federal governments. A fourth and final reason that forums are formed is for those of us who work with refugee problems to reinforce each other. Service providers usually aren't a powerful group. Most are social workers involved in the helping professions. We became political advocates out of necessity. The forum helps us define what we are and what we are doing.

Forums are good alternatives for bringing back a sense of the personal touch to probably what is dangerously becoming an impersonal system. However, some problems do exist.

If we're changing our tactics as to how to resettle the great majority of refugees - and thank goodness that there are still places where individual resettlement does occur - but if indeed the larger number of refugees are being resettled under a different model, we have to be aware of the problems that occur with that model. Among the problems that I have recognized in California, one looms especially large. There is no sense of who is in charge. In voluntary agencies, we are rather obsessed with the need to have case management or to have a case manager or even case managers.

When others are involved at a specific point in a refugee's evolution towards independence, they often become fixated on it. They fail to keep other factors, other stages - or other family members - in mind. For instance, if you're getting a refugee a job you might not know that his wife is sick and that is inhibiting him from coming to work. In California, because there is no central authority, there is often considerable difficulty in working together and in setting up different programs. The refugees get confused. They are told one thing at one agency and another thing at another agency.

One of the things I don't think we've done is to clearly identify our case loads. Refugees who have been here quite a while still keep competing for the services that are planned for new arrivals. That is one of the problems in having the private and public sectors working together. Too often, we in the private sector feel we're not taken as seriously for the part that we play in refugee resettlement and for the resources that we bring to refugee resettlement. Bureaucracies tend to only trust those within the bureaucracies. That continues to be problem for us.

Finally, we have never come to any level of established expertise in the different areas of social service for refugees. There's no context in which (or standard by which) to say this is a valid employment project, or this is a valid ESL program, or this is a valid resettlement model. Instead, we're often depending upon services that might not meet the needs in the framework or the time that we want. As a result we in the voluntary agencies might not be doing our share as expected by the other services.

Gretchen Brainerd: Our next speaker is Jean Pullen, a social worker and, as she puts it, a "bureaucrat" who has been employed by the Oregon State Department of Adult and Family Services for the past 22 years. She is currently the manager of the West Portland Branch of her department.

It is an office directly responsible for pubic assistance to refugees in the area as well as to others she calls "unloved Americans".

Jean Pullen's staff consists of a multi-ethnic polyglot crew of case workers and is one of the best in the country. She's also the former chair of the Portland Area Refugee Forum, and still sits on its board and is currently the Chairwoman of the Portland Area Refugee Service Consortium.

What can you tell us from your experience on refugees?

Jean Pullen: I am going to speak from the public sector side, but I can only really speak about my own personal experiences in the refugee program. In March 1979, I took over as the manager of the West Portland office. It is an office which serves the skidrow and chronically mentally ill population in the Portland area - essentially many homeless people as well as people who are older but not as nice as the older persons we like to think about. I also had a small group of refugee workers and we provided refugee services for all the department's clients in the county. At that time we had about 700 cases, roughly about 2200 persons were covered in that 700 caseload. Oregon only had about 5500 refugees statewide at that time. The refugee population was small and the state government was sincerely hoping that the problem would go away very quickly.

I soon discovered that there were as many different philosophies of refugee resettlement as there were volags. At that time there were five and soon the sixth volag came on the scene. Some volag directors believed that any refugee who received refugee cash assistance was considered to be immoral or at least really not very nice. My staff, who were themselves former refugees, were accused and suspected of enticing the refugees to apply for assistance: first, because it would build up a case load, and second, because they could speak to clients in their own language and third, because they explained their rights and responsibilities under the refugee assistance program. The feelings seemed to be that if a person asked for help from the federal government he/she would be tainted for life, and for course they would never get off the dole. It seems ironic that some volag directors asked me to withhold information from refugees because the truth was seen to be a threat, or at least the facts were seen to be a threat. I'll not talk about whether it is the truth or not.

I had no objections to having refugees get and maintain jobs. I heartily supported that, I still do. But I strongly objected to the morality issue. As I got to know my staff and I managed to talk with more and more of the refugees, I could see that the issues weren't that clearly defined. In the fall of 1979 and early 1980 the whole refugee population changed. Everything exploded, the boat people, the plight of the Cambodians, made the Oregonians really respond to refugee resettlement. They formed Oregonians to Save the Boat People. They did many things - there was a groundswell of community support - to get those refugees out of the camps and to get them to Oregon. They became concerned about them.

Pretty soon the refugees started arriving in Portland at the rate of 500 per month. Now, for a state our size that is a lot of people. The volags who had depended upon individual and group sponsorship found themselves scrambling for new sponsors. They found themselves not having the time to orient the new sponsors, to really train them to give help in dealing with the refugees. In many instances the sponsor-refugee relationship lasted a brief period of time. There were unreal expectations on both sides.

I know a particular sponsoring group, a church group, who found a job for the head of the household. They made certain that his wages were not paid to him because, after all, he was a 40 year old man but he was a little man so he must not be very competent (the size of the refugees was continually brought up by sponsors). He had a large family, but he didn't know how to spend his money, so they arranged to have his salary paid to the sponsors, who then doled the money out to him. Needless to say, this was done with the best of intentions, but the refugees found it to be extremely demeaning. In the particular instance I speak of the gentleman did finally lose his job - he was working at a hotel as a dishwasher - because he had problems understanding about time. It was not because he was lazy, but because he didn't even understand when they changed the shift every day. He couldn't remember when he was supposed to be at work. As soon as he applied for refugee cash assistance, the sponsors withdrew their support, saying that this was a moral issue; that if he was going to depend upon them then they would not have anything to do with him. He lost not only the sponsorship, immediate support, but the long-term support that these people could have provided as his friends.

A number of refugees have told me and members of my staff that they would rather get money from the government because they wouldn't have to continually demonstrate their thankfulness. They also felt that the government was more fair.

Then the Hmong and the Hmien begin to arrive in significant numbers. We were calling them the "Meo" and the "Yao" because that is what we had read in the literature. It took my clerk-receptionist a couple of hours of talking with some of the people to learn that these were pejoratives for them. When I first started sending documents to my State Office using these terms, I got some exasperated calls from people: "What do you mean?" "What group of people are these? They are not in the data that we have. Why are you putting them in there?" Now we refer to them correctly, but, we could have very innocently continued to offend groups of people we didn't know and there was nobody to tell us, officially, that we should not be calling them bad names.

When we had unlimited, or when it seemed there was unlimited, money for refugee assistance there was very little reason for the volags, the service providers and the governmental units to cooperate. We viewed each other with suspicion, and everybody did their own things. That was the order of the day. Refugee cash and medical assistance didn't have a time limit of course, and some refugees obviously had their own agenda - a thought that seemed to be a little startling to some of the Americans who were working with them.

We began to hire bilingual staff members at my agency just because it made sense. I felt that if refugees are to be served, they ought to be served by people who can eventually learn how to work the system themselves - work the bureaucratic system and learn how things are really done. I didn't have any mandate to do this, but it seemed to make sense.

I had to overcome the mistrust of the bureaucrats in my own state system and in fellow agencies. Some of the mistrust was spoken, a lot of it was unspoken. What they were wondering was how did I really know what the workers were saying because they could speak in their language, so they probably were telling the refugees something very different than they were telling me. That comes down to a matter of having to develop trust and, I guess, just picking good people. I do feel that I have good people, not because of my own great wisdom, but because there are good people out there.

We did form a forum in 1980 because we felt we could no longer keep fighting with each other and decided we'd better find out what is happening in the community. Everybody was taking care of a little piece of the action, each of us thinking that our own world was right there.

The first concern we addressed was the lack of educated, bilingual persons who would be willing to work for the various agencies. I felt that the people were always there, but no one had thought to hire them. We had not made it easy for them to come to our doors. In general, we found that our areas of agreement in working on refugee problems were greater than our areas of disagreement, and we had to start doing something because we were beginning to be faced with the economy and the attacks of some of the American communities that did not want refugees.

The refugees who were being sponsored by their own families or brought in by the volags then left to their own devices became a problem. This started happening about the time the weather turned very bad. We had one incident where an American landlady went to the press after she broke into the apartment where a young couple and small children were, all unconscious, suffering from pneumonia. Fortunately they did not die because she had been concerned about them and went in. They had not known that you had to order oil for heat. The oil tank was empty. No one had told them about this. She raised so much hell that the volags, private agents, everybody got on that one very fast and so did the mutual assistance associations.

The most remote issue of federal funding to the states created problems. The states and federal government often play a game of chicken: if you don't give me the money by a certain time I'm going to cut off the programs here. That is exactly what happened in Oregon in 1981, when the third quarter ended and the federal government had not given the state its appropriation for refugee cash assistance for the fourth quarter. A conscious decision was made from the governor's office and from the Director of Human Resources that we could not spend state dollars with the promise that the federal government would pay us back, because we have as much faith in the federal government as the volags have in bureaucracy. We sent out notices to the clients in their own languages advising them that as of a certain date all of the refugee cash assistance would be terminated. One 62 year old man, a Hmong gentleman and the head of a large family, who did not speak English, did not have a job and had been severely depressed, told his family he was going to commit suicide because he would be a sacrifice to the community and then the government would do something. They tried to dissuade him that weekend. He went out and hanged himself early Monday morning from a tree near his house. I heard about it at 8:00. The governor and everybody else heard about it a very short time later. This won't happen again, but it took that kind of effort on the part of somebody to bring to the consciousness of government that people in desperate straits will do desperate things (actually, the money had come the Friday night before, but I'll never convince the Hmong community that Mr. Vu's sacrifice was not the thing that brought the money back to the state).

We have a lot of help in our state from our State Refugee Coordinator. We have developed a case management system in our organization with the volags as the top priority for operating the case management system. We feel that is the wave of the future. Michael spoke about the problem of who is responsible. In Oregon, the majority of refugees live in Portland, and we have a little better control.

In Oregon, refugees themselves have worked to form their own federation and are part of the social service funding for the consortium. We know the problems are so great that we can't address them all. And we're aware that while we're serving some needs rather well, there is a whole group of refugee clients that are not being serviced. I'm talking about the older people who are housebound. I'm talking about the women with young children who are left alone while their husbands are working and their children are in school, and their children are coming home refusing to speak their own language anymore. They are speaking English now, they are Americans now, they are not going to speak their native language.

We are building up some future problems for social services and for the community as a whole, but I also think that what the refugees have brought to us has been an enrichment of our lives. My own life personally has been enriched. The community has been enriched, although the mayor of our City of Portland doesn't know that yet. I'm hopeful that the refugees will be so firmly entrenched and will become so cosmopolitan that someday he will really know how lucky we are - but I hope by that time he's someplace else. I've had the pleasure of working with very bright, creative, strong-minded people, strong-minded refugees, strong-minded volags, strong-minded bureaucrats. I find it an honor to work with them and I find that my world has expanded and is more global.

Gretchen Brainerd: Thank you Jean. Jean got into a number of important issues including the pressure of the budgetary issues and the political and social issues which are pressures on any refugee assistance resttlement program in the U.S. Karl Zukerman is now going to speak about the essential characteristics of a sound resettlement program from the perspective of the agency for which he used to work. He is an attorney who has served as the Director of Government Relations and Supportive Services of the Federation of Jewish Philanthropies of N.Y. He was the Director of the Soviet Jewish resettlement program in the U.S. He is currently the Assistant Executive Vice President of H.I.A.S., the Hebrew Immigrant Aid Society, which was created in 1880.

Karl Zukerman: I want to talk about the experience that the American Jewish comunities have had through their Jewish Federations around the U.S. in resettling about 90,000 Soviet Jews here in the last ten years, fifty thousand of which came between 1978 and 1980. It has been a very dismal scene since then, and remains so. I want to describe an optimal situation. It is not the situation which exists in the Jewish communal network, although in more places than not we're a lot closer to it than modesty would permit us to say.

First, [there is the need for] a highly integrated system of service delivery. I mean a system in which there is a regular and on-going case by case communication between a range of agencies, whether it is the family service agency, the vocational agency, the community center, the hospital that the Jewish communities sponsor or some other hospital or other health center. In any sound operation, there is a person with respect to each case who not only is its monitor but has the authority to command provision of available services. I'm not talking about wheedling, I'm not talking about convincing. I mean command. That is what I mean by case management. That seems to me fundamental. It involves commitment in this integrated system to a full range of services rather than a piecemeal set of services begging and borrowing, as it were.

Secondly, what is required is planning and coordination of that service delivery on an over-all system-wide basis. In the Jewish communal structure the Federation in each community is in the unique position to do it since it is a funding source and, for many agencies, a principle funding source for their on-going work beyond that of refugee resettlement. The Federation is in a position to use both its political and financial leverage to quickly adapt to changes.

The third item is heavy intensity of initial services, very heavy front loaded services. When we were dealing with a sufficient flow, we found it much more effective to be organizing and running our own English language program - and that, by the way, was where in many communities refugees received their cash maintenance check. If they didn't show up there they didn't get their checks. That is not traditional social work concept - but the use of such a sanction has proved to be quite effective.

Those services go into play and are operating before the refugee gets off the plane. Information about the refugee is known to the community before arrival - sometimes not much more than three days in advance, but before. In fact, information about a Soviet refugee begins to flow within about four or five days of arrival in Vienna. [When that movement was the heaviest] it was taking about six to nine months to process all the papers - and the people. We finally worked it down to a six week period. Still, within about four weeks after arrival in Vienna, the local community has a full set of information about each of its prospective arrivals. If the services were organized in a haphazard fashion, or if the agencies were overloaded, that had a negative impact on the resettlement process. But the system has come to work automatically. We now don't even think about the process that we move people through, because it just seems to go that way. There is something to be said for the one-on-one approach as opposed to the mass approach, but we would push, especially with large numbers, for a kind of automatic system that gives one the time to work with clients, rather than have to learn to negotiate the system. A lot of the time that workers spend in cajoling, or begging, or borrowing doesn't have to be spent when you have an integrated system of delivery because everybody knows that if you don't do it right away you're going to get a call from somebody who is in the position to say to you, "You were waiting for your agency's check?" That practically never had to happen because these agencies were used to working with each other in a range of service areas, not just in resettlement. They know each other personally. Sometimes one family member works in one agency, another family member works in another agency. When we're talking about one family we're talking about one family. [Editor's Note: The Jewish Federations predate by many years the refugee forums and consortiums, yet in many ways their functions are similar.]

Whatever model you see, and whatever rules you develop, you need to develop rules which clearly and consistently are presented to the clients. I could give you a long and funny lecture about dealing with a refugee group which has had to learn how, in order to survive in their country of origin, to manipulate bureaucracy like we native born Americans couldn't imagine. We were a "bureaucracy", too, and we learned how they could manipulate us because, as far as they were concerned, we were that same bureaucracy. They don't know from voluntary agencies in the Soviet Union. We learned how critical it was to be firm but not quite to the point of rigidity - feeling guilty all the way. I can't tell you anything that you don't know about the expectations of the refugees - to them the streets of America are still paved with gold. There isn't anything you can't accomplish here. Some of them have proved it rather quickly. Three years after arrival one of our refugees was already contributing to the U.J.A. campaign sums of three and four thousand dollars a year. I am talking about successful resettlement in Silicon Valley, in California, of husband and wife engineers, sixty, seventy thousand dollars of income within nine months of arrival. Clearly we are dealing with a highly trained, highly sophisticated, highly educated refugee group. These folks make the American Dream renewable.

In any event, those expectations have to be dealt with as quickly and as clearly as possible without taking the drive and the initiative out, without taking the hope out.

The sixth item is a broad base of lay support for what is essentially a professional operation. Here I want to raise a proposition for you to think about: There is an inverse relationship in the degree to which there is similarity between the arriving group and the receiving group and the need for professional, highly skillful resettlement service in the receiving community. That is, the greater the difference in cultural, ethnic, historical level of industrialization - the greater the difference between the arriving refugee group and the receiving group - the more you will need highly skilled, professionally trained people to do the service. The lay support system for our professional network is very powerful not just in terms of the dollars that it generates to support, but of the time and commitment it brings to it. That is based on a tradition of our people that goes back about 3500 years.

Briefly, I would like to mention: 1) the involvement of the emigré community itself in the process and the involvement both as a community and as relatives; 2) the fact that the Jewish community in our system put up about 60 percent of the cost of resettlement; 3) the efforts to cut down the cost of services were not an initiative to the U.S. government, they were an initiative of the Jewish community because it was paying sixty cents on each dollar being spent; and 4) those who are not refugees who have problems know that same network of services is going to be available to them for as long as they are in the community. It's not a different cast of characters. This network of services which helps resettle people in this communty is there when they have ordinary family problems, when they have ordinary parent-child difficulties, when they need some vocational re-training, etc. That's a package - optimal - but I think worth giving some consideration to if we're thinking about most effective kinds of resettlement.

Gretchen Brainerd: Thank you, Karl. I am going to turn over the floor to the discussant, Bill Sage, who is currently working for Church World Service in northern California, where there are many different types of refugee groups resettling. Prior to working for Church World Service, he was the Joint Voluntary Agency Representative in Bangkok, Thailand for four years, at the time the largest American program for the resettlement of refugees in the world. He worked nearly 11 years in Southeast Asia. His current focus is on issues surrounding secondary migration to northern California.

William Sage: For more than 12 years I have had an affiliation with many of the families who are now in this country. I have worked in Laos, and gotten to know many of the Lao, Hmong and Hmien families that settled here. Knowing them in their own country and their own environment and then seeing how they are doing at this point, I must say that I feel quite optimistic.

From the vantage point I have, the trauma of leaving the country, sitting in the camps for periods of time without much hope of knowing they were going to have to return or whether they were going to resettle in another country, and ultimately getting here and going through the essential and basic steps of resettlement is quite remarkable. They may not all be working, they may not all be earning high salaries, and they may not all be taxpayers yet, but there are an awful lot more of them who are taxpayers than is reported. I feel much more encouraged about the progress that has been made to date than much of the media would tend to lead the public to believe. Because most of the public does not have direct contact with the refugee community itself, it is difficult for them to know what is a myth and what is not. Part of my activity, and part of my efforts in many different areas and communities, is to try to bridge that gap and get some objective kind of information back into the community to help relieve misconceptions, tensions and, perhaps, help provide a little better atmosphere in which the refugee community themselves can adjust and really make a firmly rooted start in their new environs. It's hard to get baseline data, but one of the things I feel is a real injustice to the refugee communities at the present time is the great emphasis on "welfare dependency" which is being emphasized by the media and conveniently being used at this time when we're talking about re-authorization [of the Refugee Act of 1980].

However, if you take a random sampling, you'd find that in California the members of the Vietnamese population have been in California for about 4.7 years, the Cambodians for about 1.7 years. When you think about what they have been through and all they have to adjust to in order to become self-sufficient in communities where unemployment is already at the rate of 11 and 23 percent, it is not surprising that they are not all working. It takes time for a community to form a base. It takes time to have the community structure set in place so that it can help itself.

There are a number of other myths that are perpetuated in the communities, particularly in more distant and smaller communities between 25,000 and 100,000 where few services are available and where almost everyone speaks English. It is more difficult to adjust and resettle in such places, but there are still many who have stayed in those areas and have not taken the course of secondary migration to other areas. Our concern is that our [California] population now is about 220,000 Indochinese, but may I also remind you that Indochinese are not the only refugees in California. We have about 6,000 Afghan refugees that are within a very close radius of my office. We have a large Ethiopian population. We continue to accept and resettle refugees from 22 other countries into the geographical area in which we are working. And the majority are making progress. They are at different levels, but I think ultimately they are going to be very productive and they are going to be taxpayers just like everybody else. They are going to be contributing a lot more than we are giving them credit for at this point.

Now, a few comments in regard to the presentations that were made.

All of them addressed real problem areas that exist. I wanted to underscore the idea that one of the more positive aspects of the resettlement process as we know it on the West Coast, and I suspect it probably takes place in other communities as well, is the outgrowth of the forums. It has been a very useful technique and tool for coordinating.

To the four objectives mentioned by Michael Friedline and accomplishments of forums in our areas, I would also add that, because resources are becoming more difficult to obtain, the response has been to make better use of existing resources by avoiding duplication and better coordination among the different service providers in agencies. Volunteer groups have been brought in as well. The gamut of services that can be offered to assist refugees has been better coordinated.

In regard to the optimal situation of resettlement as outlined by Karl Zukerman, I think that model may work in more urbanized communities where resources are more readily available. I don't think it is an option for middle-sized or small communities where we have very small groups of a particular nationality of refugees. It is probably not a viable alternative to the kind of network that we generally have to utilize in small communities. There we have to rely upon volunteers and piece things together to come up with the best possible provisions for English training, health services, and educational and vocational opportunities.

In some communities ESL simply doesn't exist. Or, if it does, it is only one night a week. That is quite insufficient for somebody who doesn't know English, has never studied it and realizes that in order to find a job he's probably going to have to speak the language. Other resources have to be mobilized, perhaps from civic organizations who can provide volunteers on a one to one basis. It is not the most ideal situation, but I think many of us are realizing that in many communities we're going to have to piece things together from whatever resources we can possibly mobilize.

Finally, I'd like to re-emphasize Jean's comments about how the community has been enriched by the refugees themselves. I want to leave you with the thought that in spite of the fact that we're talking here about the many different issues in regard to resettlement, and that most of the issues that have been raised are in the problem areas, there are many successes. This is really the story of America.

Gretchen Brainerd: I think Bill's remarks are pertinent to what we're talking about and the emphasis on the strength of the refugee himself is very important - what it contributes to the community, what he and his family and his talents bring to our community.

Everybody on the panel agrees that it would be worthwhile to have questions from the audience, from the community at this time. The floor is open.

From the audience (unidentified): I am concerned about the acceptance of refugees who have already arrived in the camp. We had an experience with a Vietnamese woman whom we sponsored whose brother and sister were already in this country. She was picked up from her little boat by a

French boat. When she was interviewed to be accepted by the U.S. she was refused and two different agencies had two different reasons. The State Department said it was because when she answered her questions she did not give evidence of being a refugee. The ambassador in Manila, however, said that since she had been picked up by a French boat, she had to go to France. She is in France and doesn't know a soul there.

Gretchen Brainerd: This has to do with international procedure. Bill Sage can speak to this from his experience in Thailand, but if I am not mistaken the procedure is that if a boat picks up a refugee on the high seas the country whose flag that boat flies must accept the individual for resettlement. Am I correct?

William Sage: Yes, with certain exceptions. Part of the outgrowth of the conference in '79 was and agreement among 28 countries that if the flag carrier of that nation picked refugees up they would resettle them unless they had a direct or immediate relative in this country, or they had been a employee of the U.S. government previously.

From the audience (same person): It is interesting that the person from the State Department said that wasn't the reason. The real reason was that originally she didn't come out as a refugee. I think the State Department is using this kind of attitude right now, finding all kinds of reasons for reducing the number of refugees in the U.S.

William Sage: The final decisions for the U.S. programs come from I.N.S., Immigration and Naturalization Service, and consistency is a problem.

Jean Pullen: I'd like to cite something that I learned shortly before I came. There are three Cambodian children that one agency has been trying to bring into the country since last fall. They had arranged American sponsors for them, the children were essentially orphans in their own camp, though there were some relatives in this country. They were trying to bring in the children - one was a two year old baby - and they kept getting put off. Finally, we found that the two year old child had been rejected by INS because the child had not been able to articulate a well-founded fear of persecution. It took a number of calls to Washington, D.C. and to the INS officials in Bangkok to finally change it. Then they were not going to bring him in as a refugee but rather under the Orderly Departure Program which also limits the volags' ability to deal with the child. The child was finally going to arrive last week. I've heard of this from staff and refugees who are in this country and who I know are trying to get their families out. It is a real problem and we in the bureaucracies and in the volags can't even attack it without the support of the community as a whole to say this is unconscionable.

Another question asked from the floor. (It pertains to language training and cultural orientation.)

Jean Pullen: The government perspective is "You don't need to know one word of English to get a job". That is the attitude of ORR, the Office of Refugee Resettlement. My impression, and what I have heard very much in the consortium, is that it's going to take at least a month before the refugee may be able to work at all. However, there are the problems of the health screenings, social security, getting the kids in school, getting them settled, finding their way... we're talking about people who are relatively unsophisticated. I would think that probably it would take three months before they might be able to hold a job. They go into entry level jobs which are always available because people are always leaving them. Americans leave them even in times of bad economy. So, it is a matter of taking the first jobs, if they are fortunate enough to get into vocational English classes, which are specifically work related.

The attitude of the government now is that ESL should only be work specific because we don't have enough money for everybody. Attending class is never as important as taking a job and getting off the dole.

Gretchen Brainerd: Somebody from one of the voluntary agencies?

Michael Friedline: There is no set amount of time when a refugee is determined employable. It has very much to do with whole barrages of circumstances and situations, especially the abilities which he brings here. A person who comes from a European country with a marketable skill and some English ability should have no problem. A rice farmer from Cambodia would have more of a problem.

We sometimes have a tendency to punish the refugee for even utilizing the system we've created for him. When we create a system that a refugee can utilize and we give him a choice as to his own future, he is not going to take an entry level job if it offers no future when he could go to school and in a year or two take a job that has a future. Too often our response to that, to the refugees' resourcefulness for utilizing our system, is to think in terms of sanctions and punishments. I have never found those to be effective. In contrast, we ought to think in terms of incentives. For instance, if we want a refugee to go to work early why didn't we tell him that if he takes this job, he'll be put into a night time vocational program where he can raise himself up. What I hear mostly from governmental sources is, how do we sanction, how do we punish, how do we limit the refugee.

Karl Zukerman: We have been through a debate on this subject in 1979 and 1980. It had been HIAS's almost uniform practice, up until that time, to give the refugee enough training, for as long as needed, to get them as close to their previous level of employment as possible. We were frankly running a little tight of money. That is a very expensive piece of business to do. And the debate that we went through was "what is our obligation".

We came out rather clear about it. I am not saying that all of us acted on that decision, but we viewed it as an ethical obligation to continue to be available with night English classes, night vocational training or retraining, so that persons whom we had insisted take employment below a level which they ultimately would be able to handle, would not be left alone there. We would stay with them if they wanted us to do that. And it works, it works.

Gretchen Brainerd: Other questions? Bob DeVecchi is next.

Robert DeVecchi [from the floor]: I gather that the Department of Health and Human Services, HHS, is mandated under the re-authorization of the Refugee Act for a year to actively study alternative means of resettlement or so-called restructuring of resettlement, and many of you are involved in this. I think it is going to be an extremely important issue over the next year or so. My concern is that the overwhelming majority of Indochinese refugees over the past five or six years have tended to create a new class of resettlement experts whose experience comes from dealing with Indochinese and, in our usual American desire to standardize everything, our patterning of future resettlement will be based on the Indochinese experience. I wonder particularly Karl, with your agency's knowledge which goes back over the years - whether the efforts to standardize to much more of a kind of government/private oriented resettlement with x-number of months of eligibility for this and x-number of months for that, how you react to that?

Karl Zukerman: First let me quote H.L. Mencken: "For every complicated, difficult and sensitive human problem there is a direct, simple and straightforward answer that is wrong". That is the instinct of America. I think it is a human instinct to take very complex things and try to come up with a quick answer. After all our history is only 200 and some years old, and ten years to solve that problem is a big portion of our history, so we're looking for quick answers. On the other hand, one of the jobs I once had was as General Counsel to the N.Y.C. Department of Social Services. I worried about welfare fraud and so forth. There have to be rules when you're dealing with people. There have to be limits, and limits are, by definition, arbitrary. Personalized, purely personalized service, unless carried out by saints, turns out to be tyranny. So, we need to find some way to create a set of rules and expectations that are based on reality - not on the myth that there's always a lawn to be mowed by somebody the day after they arrive in the U.S. A lot of that mythology has to do with, "Oh, of course, everybody has dishes to be washed - you know that is what people should do". I think they forget that dishes are now mostly washed by machines, not by human beings. What I am saying is, you asked a very complicated question, and so because I agree with Mencken, you will get a complicated answer.

Our experience is that there is no substitute for skilled delivery of service by workers, whether they are volunteers or not. They've got to be skilled and they have to be professionally supervised. We ran an income maintenance system in the Soviet program. They didn't go to the public assistance roles. And we had very few complaints about our arbitrariness. It wasn't because the numbers we were dealing with were so small. In 1979 we had 400 workers working with 28,000 refugees. It was because, by and large, the systems that those workers were using were professionally based and very tightly supervised operations. When decisions were made they were generally - not always - explained to people. If the public welfare system were similarly functioning it could cope and it could do quite well, but it doesn't. So we find ourselves with these - by definition - arbitrary limits. I don't know the way out of that.

Dale DeHaan [from the floor]: Let me just follow up on that if I may. One is seeing now in voluntary agency waiting rooms and in the communities a different mix of people. You see Polish Catholics and refugees from Africa and the Middle East. This urge to have a single track system through which all should pass is one that rather frightens me. I notice particularly that the Afghan refugee community has to come with welfare dependence. It didn't start out that way, but it happened. Will it happen with the rather highly educated, very highly motivated Poles who are coming now? I would hope not, but are we moving in that direction in our attempts to come up with a system, a single system?

Gretchen Brainerd: Jean do you want to answer that from the public point of view?

Jean Pullen: It has only been in the last couple of years that the federal government has made a very strong statement that refugee cash assistance is not an entitlement. It is still called an entitlement program, but it is not an entitlement program as far as the government is concerned. However, to refugees coming into the country who know that the volags get money from the federal government to bring them in and who know that money is given to the states to administer them it is very hard to convince them that they are somehow immoral and less than good citizens to use things that are there so they can get themselves situated in a better job or to make a living for their family. They have not inherited the morality that to be on welfare means that you are sinful.

Gretchen Brainerd: Thank you.

PROBLEMS OF ACCULTURATION

MITZI Schroeder: We're going to talk about what I think is the most interesting and vital aspect of refugee resettlement - acculturation. Acculturation is a process of education and inner transformation, in fact, an enhancement of the individual. It is fascinating for that reason. It is vital because this transformation is necessary to the material and psychological well-being of the person trying to make a new life as a stranger in a stange land. While acculturation includes some of the basic survival skills, as, for example, knowing how to deal with a gas oven or how to get a bus - the practical matters of living in American society - it goes far beyond the basics. Acculturation can be defined as a process of reconciliation of the refugee's native culture with the culture of the adopted country. It is becoming bicultural in almost the same sense that a person becomes bilingual. It is not in any sense a wholesale adoption of the new society nor is it an abandonment of the old.

Just as we have ceased, in this country, to speak of America as a melting pot and now sometimes speak of it as a mixing bowl or a salad bowl in which many elements - some of them contradictory, some of them complementary - are blended into a new whole, so we can look upon the process of acculturation as a blending of the elements of the old and the new values of the home and the host country.

During the acculturation process the refugee must learn that old behaviors and old ways of expressing himself may have very different meanings in the new culture. He must learn this not because his old values are in any sense wrong, but because they may have a meaning which may be not understood in the new society. In a very real sense the process of acculturation is learning to understand cultural information that is heard, seen and learned and, in turn, to communicate in new cultural terms.

The process of acculturation itself is very difficult and very frustrating. It is filled with anxiety. Failure can be devastating. It can lead to the individual's psychological paralysis, isolation and depression. But successful acculturation leads to the enrichment of the individual just as learning a new language is a process of enrichment.

Perhaps we didn't realize that acculturation was quite so important in the resettlement process until the influx of the Indochinese population in 1975. As has been brought out in some of the presentations today, many people from non-Western cultures came to this country in a very short period of time. Often they were settled in communities where there was no group from the same country to assist them in learning about their new society. Therefore, the resettlement community and individual Americans began to realize that some help was needed in bridging the gap between the old culture and the new. As a result, many formal and informal cultural orientations or ("C.D." programs as is sometimes called) were formed.

Our first speaker will be discussing the process of acculturation and also some of the barriers to it. Stephanie Newman is the director of programs in the Resource Development Department of the Federation of Jewish Philanthropies in New York. Her agency is involved in the planning and coordination of services to Soviet Jewish refugees, including employment counseling, vocational training and re-training, individual and family counseling and the whole range of services that are related to cultural orientation. She is also involved in many committees on policymaking and reviewing issues regarding services to refugees and new immigrants as well as other immigration issues.

Stephanie Newman: Thank you. One of the advantages (or disadvantages) of going later in the program, is that much of what you have decided to say has already been said. It will make my remarks shorter than I had planned.

As was already said, there is a problem about talking about problems all the time. I had a problem with the title of this particular session, "Problems of Acculturation", because I think when we focus so much on the problems, we fail to take into perspective the successes that happen.

I prefer to think about the refugee groups that we work with as having particular characteristics that we have to learn about, that we have to acculturate to. We have to learn their customs, their mores, and their norms to a certain extent. We have to change in a certain way, too, so that they can be aided in a process of acculturation in our society. I would rather not think of it as a problem orientation, but rather how we may work together. However, I do like the overall title of this conference, "Working with Refugees", because that, in fact, is what we do, we work together.

What I can talk about is our experience in New York with the Soviet Jewish refugee population, which represents almost 50 percent of those from the USSR who have come into the U.S. In the last session one of the questions that was asked was "Can the experiences in the Indochinese refugee program be applicable to other groups?"

I would suggest that even when we're working with those from a single country or particular region, we have to remember that it is seldom a single population. In the Soviet Jewish Program we have to bear this in mind, too, because despite the fact that the people are all coming from the Soviet Union, they are not all the same.

There are at least four distinct groups of people who come to the U.S. from the Soviet Union. Each brings their own cultural background and we must be prepared to recognize these differences in the programs offered and in the kinds of expectations that we have.

Most of the refugees who come here are from what has been described as the 'heartland' of the Soviet Union, that part of the Soviet Union that has been part of the U.S.S.R. since the revolution, since 1917. These are the people who have been most indoctrinated in the Soviet system. There are others, though, who come from areas of the Soviet Union that were not incorporated until 1939 or 1940 or until after World War II. Their experience is somewhat different. In addition, there are some who come from the Central Asian area of the Soviet Union. They are called Bukharin Jews and their main language is not Russian, but a derivative of the Iranian national language, Farsi. There are also Soviet Jews who come from Georgia. Their main language is Georgian.

Within this particular population group there are certain characteristics that we in New York and across the country had to become aware of as we get involved in the resettlement program and began to look at the issue of acculturation.

Karl Zukerman said earlier that the Soviets who come here are wonderful at manipulating the system. The reason this is so is because there isn't trust in the government in the Soviet Union. One doesn't believe what one hears from the government. To survive, one manipulates, one argues. Laws are made to be broken. We sometimes have a great deal of difficulty in understanding that when we first come into contact with the refugee population.

In addition, the whole issue of authority versus freedom is critical. Our experience in New York is that many Russians see our system as very loose. For example, adolescents are amazed at what they are allowed to get away with in school.

We must also understand friendship. Friendship in the Soviet Union is terribly important. When one doesn't trust authority, and one doesn't trust government, the people that you trust are close friends. That is where you get your information; that is where you can be open; that is where you can be loose. Americans have a problem with that in certain ways. While we like to think of ourselves as friendly people, we tend to be friendly in a context that is somewhat superficial. We don't open our homes up in the same way as the Soviets might. The Russians expect to be invited to peoples' homes once there is an indication of friendship. They expect to share confidences; they expect to get certain kinds of information.

Most of services for the Soviet Jews are not in a separate resettlement agency, they are part of our existing system. For the acculturation process itself, the most important agency is our community center.

The community center is where people come for general group activities - clubs, recreation, cultural activities. In New York there are 14 neighborhoods where the Russians have settled. In the neigborhoods where service centers exist we have seen the greatest success in acculturation. Just before I came here I called one of our neighborhood service centers. Without any prompting on my part, the director told me, "The thing that I want to accomplish this year is moving our neighborhood service center into the community center because I'm finding that the people living in our community want to engage in activities with the native born population". They are beginning to see themselves as part of our community. I must tell you, though, that everything is not good. There are some significant problems of acculturation at this point in time.

There are three major groups that are having visible problems. One group in particular consists of those people who have not been able to get jobs that are equivalent to the jobs they had in the Soviet Union. This is very important because status is conferred in the Soviet Union not by material things, but by the positions people hold. One of the reasons we have so much difficulty in getting the Soviet Jews to accept the first job offered is that often it is not equivalent to the one held in the Soviet Union. Accepting means lowering one's status. In addition, there are many people who can't find any work, as I am sure is the case in other refugee communities. When they do manage to find a job they are highly vulnerable. As the last hired they are the first fired. Job related problems are the most serious ones that we see as the cause of people seeking mental health services in our agencies.

The second group having severe problems acculturating is the teenagers. Being a teenager in any society is not easy. But being uprooted at that point in time, being transplanted into a culture that is so different from the one that you have been brought up in, causes very special difficulties. We're seeing acting out. We're seeing truancy. We're seeing drug addiction and sexual promiscuity. Some of this sounds like what we see in the native born population of teenagers. However, Russian teens do these things for different reasons than American youth. They do it because of their problems with the looseness of American society.

The third group having extreme difficulty in adapting is the elderly. I am not sure that there will ever be much success in most of the elderly really learning the new customs, mores and norms of our society. What we have tried to do for them is not to have acculturation as a goal, but to enable them to function within their own society, with one another, and we have helped them to organize a city-wide self-help organization.

Let me briefly return to the necessity of understanding different groups. Not doing so is one of the most serious barriers to aiding in the acculturation process. We see it in the American Jewish community.

The American Jewish community had certain expectations of the Soviet Jews when they came here. We expected them to be certain kinds of people, and we expected them to be grateful for our assistance in bringing them here. We expected them to be religious and to be active in the religious community and, much to our surprise, they didn't turn around and thank us enough for helping them to get here. They did not necessarily become active members of synagogues. That is our problem; it is not their problem. We have to understand that they will identify as Jews in the way they are comfortable with, and they will participate in Jewish community activities in the way they choose to participate, in the same way that Jews who are part of the American Jewish community do.

Mitzi Schroeder: I think Stephanie has made some very interesting points. She did echo something I said earlier, that acculturation is a process that enriches both the individual and the community, but she went beyond that to say that the process itself necessitates a degree of understanding not only on the part of the refugee, but also on the part of those in the resettlement programs.

We are going to move on now to hear from Michael Huynh, who is well qualified to speak from both sides of that street, if I may put it that way. Michael is of Vietnamese origin. He is the Executive Director of the Center for Southeast Asia Refugee Resettlement in San Francisco. He has studied at Berkeley and at the University of San Francisco, and has degrees in Public Administration and Business Administration. He is now the chairman of the San Francisco Refugee Forum.

Michael Huynh: Thank you for your kind words. Actually I was very reluctant when Peter Rose called me and asked me to come to this conference. I said to myself, "Well, I would be at one of the fanciest colleges in the country. My English is ... it would mean that I have to speak perfect English." I didn't think I could do it. But out of Peter's kindness of wanting me to be acculturated, I accepted the invitation. So please bear in mind that I am only half acculturated. If my accent or pronunciation prevents you from understanding what I am trying to say, then I will be available after my presentation.

At the same time that Peter Rose asked me to come to this conference, the first bilingual Vietnamese magazine asked me to write an article about problems of acculturation. I like what I wrote, so I am going to repeat it to you today.

The immigration of refugees has become a major national issue. Increasing numbers of refugees coming to the U.S. and the state of the national economy have created an environment in certain locales which become extremely critical of the continued in-migration of refugees. The fact that substantial numbers of refugees in the last decade have come from Asia rather than Western Europe has created an environment which makes the refugee appear even more obtrusive. Because the U.S. is basically a Western country, Asians are far more recognizable than Europeans. This distinction also makes for hasty and inadequate judgments about the nature of the Southeast Asian Refugee. The receiving communities' reaction to the refugee and his/her reaction to this reaction will be the subject of my thoughts today.

In *The Sentimental Imperialists* by Thompson, Stanley and Perry, there is a particularly compelling passage which describes America as a country which imagines itself as an entirely open society, taking to its bosom the peoples of the world, while at the same time being able to systematically define out of existence the reality of Asia as a separate and rich culture which, through its immigrants, has added to the richness of culture in America. Asia has been described by some as a civilization which is basically defective, despotic and stagnant. Others describe Asia as a backward culture. By thus portraying Asia, it becomes easy to pass judgment without clearly understanding the reality of the many diverse cultures in the region.

With the movement of so many refugees at one time into the U.S., generalizations were easily attached to the newly-arrived groups. Most of the generalizations reflected back upon the preconceptions which were based upon little or no real knowledge of Asian people. Confusion resulted from the first encounters between refugees and Americans. Regardless of where the refugee was, certain prejudgments were made which reflected an idealized version of the refugee, without much appreciation of the culture from which the refugee came, the circumstances which placed the refugee here, and any sensitivity as to how the refugee might imagine him/herself now that he/she was in America.

The fact that to this day most Americans have difficulty distinguishing between the cultures of Asia, and the fact that Americans place Asians in a single culture context even though there is no central cultural core in Asia but rather a diversity of rich cultures which have intermingled at points in history but remained culturally distinct, creates a major hurdle for the Southeast Asian refugee to jump once he/she arrives in the U.S. Because Asian refugees are different, they bear witness to their differentness and have no intention of doing otherwise. Americans have difficulty in integrating them into their fairly superficial preconceptions of who and what Asians are and should be.

Regardless of the efforts made by individuals, groups and the government, it is ultimately left to the refugee to change these views. In the mid-seventies, when the economy was fairly healthy and the refugees who arrived during this period had significant numbers of cultural contacts with Americans at the administrative level, the refugee found it possible to integrate into American culture. However, as the economy has grown more fragile and the newly-arrived refugees are less experienced and sophisticated in the Western way, it has become more difficult for them to progress from dependent refugees to independent citizens. The result has been the growth of ghettos in the impacted areas where the refugees develop ways of encapsulating themselves rather than reaching out and integrating themselves into the overall society. A growing number of refugees have chosen to remain within an environment which is culturally supportive, rather than brave the cultural insensitivity of the host culture.

Because American society is experiencing a period of stress in its economic development, and recently-arrived refugees lack basic skills and cultural approbation, many refugees have found it difficult to secure employment. Therefore, more and more of them are forced into a dependency cycle which reduces the pressure to adapt, along with destroying any motivation for them to make a successful transition from one reality, "home", to another reality, "America". Given the decreased resources allocated to refugee resettlement, the increasing numbers of the residual refugee population seeking shelter on welfare, and the lack of interest by the American people in seeing refugees integrated into the society, it is becoming more and more difficult to help the refugees' transition from dependence to independence.

What is needed? First, a realization that refugees are not one of a piece, that they represent highly diverse cultural backgrounds and realities. Second, that refugees were not merely shipped over to America, that they were literally forced out of their countries, that they had to brave many kinds of indignities to reach the U.S., that to decide to leave, to go through the rigors of displacement and persecution both at home and in resettlement camps, they had to be highly motivated to succeed. Each of them, in his/her own way, was extremely motivated to succeed.

Acculturation for the refugee, then, is not a matter of sweeping them under the rug with systems of support which ignore history and humanity, hoping that one day they will re-emerge as full-fledged "Americans". Rather, they need first to be appreciated as culturally separate, individually seeking their own futures, and highly motivated to succeed at becoming a part of this society without giving up or disowning their past. With this appreciation should come the realization that acculturation of such a large number is not something which will happen rapidly. The process of acculturation can begin by identifying the refugees as representing different and rich cultural groups, and not amenable to the traditional systems used for the support of the poor citizens in this country. Building a system which emphasizes methods which will capitalize on the motivation to succeed without endangering the maintenance of support of the family will surely help in the process of acculturation. It is doubtless that refugees represent extremely active and positive citizen material. However, to treat them as misfits or miscreants will only reduce the ability of the society to use the energy and power they represent for the future.

Mitzi Schroeder: Thank you Michael. We are now going to move on to Peter Pond, the Director of Refugee Resettlement for the Lutheran Service Association of New England. Peter also served in Thailand in 1979 and 1980 on the Thai Committee for Refugees, helping to re-organize Buddhist Temples and Buddhist cultural groups in Thailand. He is a minister of the United Church of Christ, and he characterizes himself as an 'international community organizer' who has worked in a number of countries on such projects as organizing indigenous Peace Corps-like groups.

Peter Pond: At the end of the last session, I had a question. It relates in an indirect way to this discussion. It is a deep concern about the professionalism (Bob DeVecchi said 'standardization', I would say 'specialization') of the refugee resettlement strategy - or business - which is invalidating to the refugees, and invalidating to the grass-roots community supports. In New England, we often have church sponsors but we can also have any group of people who care. I see this as a big issue with all kinds of relationships aside from acculturation, for instance, political overtones. It's very difficult as more and more of the energy goes from grass roots to professional. We're paid by the federal government and we can't be as supposedly involved in advocacy.

This is related to one of the first questions I wish to raise about the whole issue of acculturation. That is, it deals with, at the very gut level, the professional's disdain of the non-professional. I am really not a "refugee professional". My experience has been limited to Cambodians in this country in the last couple of years. One of the events we watched in the last year was the MAA [Mutual Assistance Association] development project, the cluster development project. I thought the notion of government, volags, churches and community offering resources to the Cambodian community to develop leadership to empower them to help themselves was terrific. Obviously, the Cambodians weren't professional refugee resettlement workers. Obviously, Cambodians came with enormous "brokenness" from having participated in an Auschwitz-like genocide. They didn't trust Americans - or each other. And so, to begin with a goal of having an indigenous leadership development program, and not to recognize that there are going to be problems like non-professionalism was absurd. I felt that volags were disdainful of the effort, were not supportive of the attempts to work, were super-critical of Cambodian workers coming late or fighting with each other. I thought this was a bad chapter in acculturation because certainly ten years from now the Cambodians, like everybody else, are going to have to be doing refugee resettlement for themselves. And certainly there can be no more important goal for all of us than to figure out ways, painful as they may be, [for them], non-professional as they may be, to develop themselves, to organize themselves on all levels - whether it is on the level of helping people to develop institutional strength, to be able to report money to their own community or to be able to have boards of directors. I thought, by and large, that we were, as non-Cambodians, as volags, disdainful. We must now figure out ways to use our resources, money and time to help MAA's develop, or help Buddhist temples develop or help indigenous study institutes.

We now have a New England Khmer Studies Institute. It's not well organized, but it's a major committment of ours to work with it, to support it.

The second problem I raise to you is a religious problem, and it has to do with those religious volags like the one to whom I take most of my cases, LIRS [The Lutheran Immigrants and Refugee Service] - the whole question of invalidating the past by being evangelical. From Thailand in 1979 to today, one of the acculturation strategies of the children was that, when the religious volag operated the children's center in Sakaeo during the day [they] would wear a cross. But at night, when we would bring the Buddhist monk, they would turn the chain around and there would be a Buddha. It was survival. We need to find ways, as for myself, a Christian, to not hide from what I am, yet to find a way to be what I am without invalidating the rich Buddhist past, a way even to realize what Pol Pot did in killing 80,000 Buddhist monks in trying to exterminate that richness, and the brokenness which that experience brings to people. Obviously their willingness to switch the chain around and to be 'Christian' is in order to please, but how invalidating, how opposite it is from empowering somebody in the process.

Last, I raise an issue which is a very personal one. I have six Cambodian children in my home. One of the arguments we would have with Zia Risvi and his staff in 1979 and 1980 in Thailand was that it was not necessarily so that everybody coming to the U.S. as unaccompanied minors would want to try to go back. How do we, in the whole strategy of acculturation, validate my children - Cambodian children, Vietnamese children - who want to say to their sponsor, to their volags, to this country "Thank you, but I want to go back to my country". In our family we struggle with this, and sometimes at different spaces everybody hopes someday to go to college, to someday go back and make peace in Cambodia. How did we, in the whole strategy of acculturation, validate somebody who wants to go back and reclaim their country ten or fifteen years from now?

Mitzi Schroeder: Thank you Peter. We'd like to open the discussion up to questions from the floor now.

Question from floor regarding competition among various groups.

Michael Huynh: I don't know about other parts of the country, but I don't believe that there is that kind of competition in San Francisco. I think San Francisco - California - is unique because there are a lot of Asians there. So, by having refugees living in that area, I don't feel that yet. I don't know where you get that information from, that tension exists between Asians and non-Asians.

First questionner, continuing to press idea of resistance to newcomers.

Michael Huynh: Actually, I don't blame them for feeling [put upon by the influx of new refugees]. I think it is our fault not to tell people - native Americans - of why we are here. You who work in this field know why we are here because of your involvement in Vietnam, and I want you to know that back in 1945 more than two million Vietnamese died of starvation. None of us then left Vietnam. It was only after you were involved with us, with all your promises, that we came here. To listen to those comments that we are stealing jobs from native Americans, especially at this time, is very hard. As one of the assemblymen I know in San Francisco told me, "Michael, you are only one notch above the prisoners. That is our priority in this society."

Peter Pond: Bayard Rustin, when he came back about a year and a half ago from a trip to Thailand organized by IRC, said, "Gee, the blacks all over this country are saying 'What the hell are you doing talking about the problems in Thailand, of Vietnamese and Cambodian refugees, when 50 percent of the black teenagers are unemployed.' I say to them any country that turns its back on them, on the destruction of people such as these, will turn its back on the blacks too." It's worthwhile having answers for the people in your hometown who feel that way, it's worthwhile thinking about some of those kinds of thoughts of Bayard Rustin.

Michael Huynh: I feel there is a failure of the volags to develop leadership in our communities. As someone just said, refugees have to take care of themselves in the future. I do not know much about a cluster project to really make a comment on that.

Eve Burton of ICM [from floor]: asks about "cluster resettlement".

Mitzi Schroeder: I can make a comment on that. Cluster resettlement is something that we in resettlement aren't doing, it's being done by the refugees themselves. We haven't really gotten into the question of secondary migration very much in this conference so far. But, of course, when people are placed in communities remote from fellows of their own ethnicity, they often do move to places where they can find people with whom they share a language, with whom they share religion, celebration of holidays and customs, so that they can develop their own support system. It is because we have begun to realize this that cluster resettlement is being given more attention. At the same time, with the early large influx of Vietnamese there was a tendency to try to spread the incoming refugees out in as many communities as possible so as to try to maximize access to community resources as far as voluntary help and support.

Peter Pond: There were some marvelous models of Khmer caring for Khmer. They didn't call it case management. There is a problem in turning an American social service system into an indigenous social service system and expecting the same job description. In those camps, the temple was a place where laymen and women and monks did those things. Now, obviously, this is difficult to do here, but we can be perhaps a little more adaptive and look for more traditional ways. Indigenous groups are teachers, counselors, maybe not case managers. I am not sure that it is simply a matter of taking our job description and hiring indigenous people. I think we also need to develop self-help systems which have some tradition to them, and then there are skills.

Mitzi Schroeder: I'd also like to add something to that. While I do agree with the gentleman who made the comment that much more is needed in the way of opportunities, training and exposure to management skills for representatives of the various refugee communities and refugee programs, it is not the case that this is not happening to some extent. Speaking for the U.S. Catholic Conference, we have between 140 and 160 active resettlement offices in the country, and there is hardly one which does not have, or has not had periodically, ethnic staff working as case workers and as supervisors and even working as directors of those programs. We have a program now where every month we send at least one or two of these workers to the camp in the Philippines for a one month period to work in the overseas ESL and orientation program as a benefit to that program, but also as part of our staff building efforts. Other volags are also doing similar things. This is happening more slowly than it should, but it is certainly something that I think we can build upon for the future.

Stephanie Newman: In our program in New York at the height of the program 24 agencies were involved in the Soviet Jewish resettlement program. When we began we wanted to be sure we had, at the very least, Russian speaking workers on the staff, and, if possible also have people from the Russian community who were already here on the staff of our agencies. It wasn't very easy to accomplish at the beginning, but at this point every one of our agencies has people from the Soviet Jewish community on the staff. Many of them are the heads of programs.

I'd like also to make a comment on self-help. While I said that we have encouraged self-help, we were at fault when we started helping the Soviet Jewish community in developing self-help mechanisms because we Americans have a certain concept of what self-help is. We expected the community to organize self-help groups along our model. That was not possible because of what the nature of the group means to Soviets; what groups are and how they are run. We had to learn that ourselves. It has taken a self-help group of Russian older adults one year to develop their by-laws and structures and to elect officers. It has been a terribly difficult struggle, but it is a tremendous accomplishment. The major problem is not with the group itself, the major problem is with those people who are evaluating it. The funding sources, foundations and the Federation itself are saying, "Is this all that they have accomplished in a year?"

Mitzi Schroeder: I think that might be a good note on which to close. I'd like to thank the panelists and all of you who have participated with your questions and Peter Rose for bringing us all together here today.

THE MEANING OF VOLUNTARISM

PETER Rose: About four months ago, a number of the people who are in this audience gathered in the Smith College Chapel to pay homage to a man who had touched more people's lives than anyone I have ever known. His name was Simon Shargo. I would like to tell you some of the things I said at the memorial service so you, too, can get a better sense of the man we honor at this conference.

Simon wasn't a scholar in the formal sense of that term, nor was he a writer of learned articles, nor was he a professor. Yet it seemed especially fitting for those of us who were there to remember him on a college campus because he was a serious student, a student of human nature. He was also a faithful correspondent, an accomplished musician, an artist and a teacher of many subjects.

Simon Shargo taught little children to play the piano. And, in his later years, not very long ago, he entered a classroom in this very building to tell our students what it meant to spend a lifetime helping others face what he himself had known, the experience of exile. Robert Frost might have been speaking of Simon Shargo when he wrote: "My object in living is to unite my vocation with my avocation as my two eyes make one in sight". Simon's vocation and avocation were caring. Caring for others. Caring about others.

Born nearly 90 years ago in Nicoliev, in the Ukraine, Simon was the son of a revolutionary and the grandson of the *shamus*-or sexton-of the largest synagogue in Odessa. He was in some ways the combination of both men, his father and grandfather. He was an unstinting fighter for universal justice. He was a person deeply committed to the Jewish community. Early in his life, his training in agronomy and economics were put to work when he served as an aide to the Herbert Hoover American Emergency Relief Administration in Russia. He also worked as an agent for those who were helping to establish Jewish agricultural settlements in the Ukraine.

There, in his native land, he witnessed the challenges to the old order; the raging conflicts between the Whites and the Reds; the plots and counterplots; the purges and the terrible suffering of the Russian people. He knew loneliness when his beloved father was exiled to Siberia for his activities in the Socialist Revolutionary Party.

In the early 1920s, with the Bolsheviks back in power, the Shargos left their homeland forever. They had intended to come to the United States, but stayed on in Berlin where, within a very short time, Simon became a field representative for the refugee agency you now know as the American Jewish Joint Distribution Committee. He was to remain with that organization for over fifty years, moving, as was necessary during the terrible days of ascendant Nazism, from Berlin to Paris, then from Paris to Marseilles, and eventually to Geneva where he lived until the mid-1970s. His work as Director of Finance for the Joint put him in the center of pre-war attempts to assist Jews in escaping from Germany and the occupied lands, to provide relief for those who managed to get out and, later to aid in the resettlement of thousands upon thousands of displaced persons.

Simon Shargo bore witness to man's inhumanity to man. He tried to stem the tide. He tried to aid the "tempest-tost". He was involved in every conceivable plan to rescue those called the "saving remnant".

He could speak of "the voyage of the damned" not as an abstract exercise in book reviewing, but from personal experience, for he knew the role of the Joint in trying to aid those aboard the ill-fated S.S. St. Louis. He could tell of heart-wrenching debates about making pacts with the devil himself in the hopes to exchange trucks and machinery for human beings incarcerated in camps inside Europe. He could and did relate tales of heroism and sacrifice as well as stories of complicity and dishonor. He could name names. Simon Shargo had seen what fellow human beings could do and did do to each other.

But Simon could also take the greatest pride in how his agency raised millions of dollars to help find places of refuge for the dispossessed and how it assisted in establishing a homeland for the homeless. He marveled at how a few stalwart souls were willing to work unstintingly for the good of so many. He often spoke of the strength of the human spirit, individuals such as his beloved friend whom some of you knew - Charlie Jordan - who embodied so much of what was true, what was good, what was brave.

As Simon grew older he had many misgivings about the directions in which the politicians in Israel were heading, but he remained a Zionist. He expressed concern about the ease with which young minds could be swayed by Utopian promises, but he remained an optimist. He saw beauty in religious ritual, in the celebration of faith, but it was man's action rather than God's word that continued to intrigue him most. Simon remained a humanist. He loved music; he loved art; he loved books. But most of all he loved people - his immediate family, Nelly and her son and daughter, his grandchildren and, as I said at the memorial service, his extended family which included us all.

As some of you know, I spent hours with the man who was locally known as "Noona", first in Geneva and later in his apartment on Harrison Avenue and in my office in Wright Hall, trying to get him to tell his story and the story of others with whom he worked in the field of caring for refugees. The conversations we had would last for hours, interrupted only by his scurrying back to the kitchen to make more tea, and inevitably prolonged by his desire to tell me just one more anecdote about one acquaintance of his or another. Each was, as he would always put it "extra-ordinary". So, of course, was he.

That November day we honored the indomitable spirit of the man who some of you knew in this town as the "Mayor of Harrison Avenue". At this special conference on "Working with Refugees" we honor his life's work.

In a letter that I received the other day accepting the invitation to join us, Zia Risvi, the regional representative of the U.N. High Commission for Refugees whom you heard speak this morning, said, "I see that Sheppie Abramowitz will be delivering the Memorial Lecture. It will be a pleasure to see her and so many other friends again in an environment quite different from the refugee camps where we worked together." At the time they worked together, along with Lionel Rosenblatt, Bill Sage and many others you have met the last few days, Mr. Risvi was the UNHCR's regional coordinator for Southeast Asia. Sheppie Abramowitz was an energetic worker with the Joint Voluntary Agency in Thailand, and especially with KEG, the Khmer Emergency Group. Sheppie was in Thailand because her husband was the U.S. Ambassador. Morton Abramowitz was a man who made the plight of the Indochinese refugees a primary concern during his tenure in that post, a man who, I believe, more than any other American official pressed his host country, his own country, and many other governments to deal compassionately and effectively with the hundreds of thousands who crowded the border camps along the Mekong in the North to Songkhla in the South, and especially those on the Thai-Cambodian border.

Sheppie was not and is not the stereotypical ambassador's wife, Hollywood style. She is an ambassador herself, representing to me and to many of us the highest ideals of this country.

Sheppie was born in Baltimore, received her B.A. from Bryn Mawr. After graduation she worked on the Hill in Washington, married Mort, who was an East Asia specialist, and went back and forth from Asia to Washington where she worked for then-Senator Muskie, became a lobbyist for a number of universities including the State University system in California, and went back overseas. When she was in Hong Kong she joined the International Rescue Committee, an organization that is also represented here by Bob DeVecchi.

I asked Sheppie how she got involved with refugees. She explained that it wasn't just through Mort, or mainly through Mort, but because her mother had been a worker with HIAS, the Hebrew Immigrant Aid Society which we heard about this afternoon in Karl Zukerman's talk.

THE MEANING OF VOLUNTARISM

In Thailand, Sheppie worked with Indochinese refugees on the border between Thailand and Cambodia with the Khmer Emergency Group until she and Mort returned to Washington. She became the liaison for the family unit in the State Department. She is leaving in a few days for Vienna where her husband is now the U.S. Delegate to the Conventional Arms Talks, and hopes to do refugee work there.

I am delighted that Sheppie is with us.

Sheppie Abramowitz: I thank you very much for asking us to participate in this conference. Mort and I were both flattered to be asked. Although Peter has been very generous, reminding me that he invited me on my own, we all know that I wouldn't have been in Thailand without Mort, although I do believe that in our family I was the first to be interested in refugees. When we were in Hong Kong he was a consular official. I don't even know if he knew what I was doing with IRC.

I wanted to talk a little about the role of volunteers in the refugee crisis. I did some research on Mr. Shargo, and found that he was, in a sense, a volunteer throughout his professional life. In addition to his own job with the AJJDC, he carried what his friends called a personal caseload of hundreds of refugee cases in support and aid. He personally became involved in these cases that were quite beyond what he was doing for AJJDC. The example of his personal volunteerism will hopefully sustain us all in this period now where there is a declining interest in the refugees.

Volunteerism is sort of the vogue these days, and I am reluctant to talk about it because I don't quite like the way it is being bandied about. Next month we're going to have National Volunteer Week, and President Reagan said television should start showing more of the volunteers on the 7:00 news. I really have never seen volunteerism as a substitute for the role of international agencies, or voluntary agencies, or the U.S. government, or the host government in a refugee crisis. Volunteers, however, do add special qualities and attitudes in a crisis less perhaps for what they actually do in the field than for the support that they generate.

It was very clear in Thailand. There volunteers built support for the efforts to deliver services to refugees. Volunteers built support in finding long-term solutions for refugee problems. Volunteers became advocates for the interest in refugees both in the host country and in resettlement countries. Volunteers contributed in the area of public education for refugee needs and concern. Support, advocacy and public education are links forged by volunteers between the refugee and the private and public agencies and between the public and the refugees.

Now, my views are limited by the experiences that we had in Hong Kong and, more recently, in Thailand. But, especially today, I learned again that my views are reinforced by hearing about other refugee experiences. We learned a lot in this Indochina escapade that we were all on, and I am going to talk of what we learned about volunteers.

Volunteers linked us to the support network at home. They were the constituency builders. They were the people that stimulated political support and financial support. There was a real connection between the number of volunteers we had out in the field and the amount of interest generated in the United States, initially for the boat people and then for the Khmer. There was a direct correlation between the volunteers' first hand experience and support for resettlement, particularly with returning doctors and nurses. There was a direct link between the enthusiasm of the volunteer and the raising of money for agency programs. These links are really very important and may be the most important contribution we get from volunteers, and in a crisis they are links to value and sustain. When we discourage the volunteers, the links weaken.

One of the additional roles that expatriate volunteers have in the field (and this is not an original thought - it is really a thought from Mark Brown) is that the volunteer is a credible witness and a protector. In the field the expatriate volunteer is a credible witness to what is going on, and there are sometimes things going on around that aren't very pleasant. There is injustice. There is neglect. There are mistakes on the part of the agencies, the bureaucrats, the relief agencies, and usually the volunteer sees it all and tells it all too - usually to the press. Nevertheless, that is a vital element in keeping the effort on track and in keeping us honest in the field. In spite of the fact that many volunteers gave press conferences on arrival and on departure, overall I insist that the expatriates played an essential part in keeping the effort, in a sense, honest.

Most of the controversies in the field at the time were about rape, unaccompanied minors, birth control, the amount of medication and brutality which were initially seen and reported by expatriate volunteers. It is fortunate that they were there as witnesses because people who are out in the field for a long time become innured to some of that and may not see it at all.

When volunteers first arrived we were delighted and eager for their outpouring of energy and sympathy. We encouraged them to come and in those first moments never wondered why they came. We needed them, especially in the first weeks of the Khmer crisis, when we actually needed extra hands. If I was giving I.V.s they were really short-handed because I knew nothing about I.V.s!

During that time we saw a variety of volunteers - doctors, nurses, teachers, housewives, students, professors, business people, world travelers, reporters - all kinds of people. I am sure some of these volunteers have popped up in Honduras and various other places since then. We went out to get volunteers and had plenty around. The press and television helped.

When we're dealing in such a highly emotionally charged atmosphere, and when you see the physical discomfort that most of the volunteers have to undergo, you begin to wonder why people went out there in the first place. People came to work in Thailand for a variety of reasons. Some of them were ambulance chasers - or "crisis junkies". I still see some of those people; they still come to see me. Some people came because they were unemployed, or were seeking converts. Some had lived in

Cambodia before '75 and had a link to Cambodia. Some wanted to know about tropical medicine. Some wanted to write a book. Some wanted to take photos. There were lots of reasons people ended up out there. It became hard not to question their motives, and it became hard to work with certain volunteers if you disagreed with their intentions or their points of view.

The lesson we learned from that experience is a lesson I certainly learned the hard way - that you shouldn't worry about the motives of the volunteers. In fact, you'd better not worry too much about your own motives for being out there.

The problem was, were we getting the job done in those few months? Were we utilizing the volunteers in a good way? Were we allocating the resources sensibly? Were we integrating the volunteers into some on-going enterprise? The questions about why these people came were really questions that should have just been dropped. It took me a while to catch on that it was a tiresome exercise. Most of the large agencies in the field were quite surprised by the large number of people who landed in Thailand.

If the volunteer had been recruited at home by an agency, there was a chance that there was a real job for him to do in the field. If the volunteer landed in Thailand with no affiliation, it became difficult to integrate that volunteer to the task. In fact, Lionel Rosenblatt made me the volunteer handler because he thought that if we didn't have something for these volunteers to do they would feel better if I'd give them tea and chocolate chip cookies and invite them to lunch at the Ambassador's residence. And I did it.

The international agencies found the effective use of volunteers to be almost beyond their grasp because volunteerism is really an American phenomenon. They never saw the link between support and volunteers. On one hand, the volunteers were treated with absolute disdain, and on the other hand the agencies were conducting international appeals for funds. They didn't see that they weren't going to be able to mobilize funds for political support or donations of material if they couldn't utilize their volunteers better.

In many cases they actively discouraged donations of time, money or peoplepower, which I thought was a very unfortunate occurrence. Even if you have to put the medicine in a store-house, I think you should accept it because it is building up some links to keep the effort going. Agencies, public and private, must have volunteer coordinators who anticipate, coordinate and enlist peoplepower in a crisis. Coordinators must be planners and managers of human resources. Training the volunteers before they leave their home country is essential.

Volunteers do have to be sensitized as to the political atmosphere in the first-asylum countries. They must know the mores of the country where they are going. Volunteers have to adhere to the customs of the country and the rules laid down by the host country, and by the people who are running the camps. It is very hard for us to understand that. We blame the volunteers, but we didn't bother telling them that they shouldn't be going around in shorts, for instance.

While not involving ourselves in the motivations of our volunteers, we must prepare ourselves to utilize them effectively. We must prepare them to work effectively and we must be prepared to insist that volunteers adhere to the guidelines worked out by the agencies in the host countries.

I now want to highlight a number of areas that remain important for people, for the personal attention of volunteers, as well as for the professional refugee agency community. They are not all new ideas.

As we know, there are always going to be refugees and there will always be crises in different regions on a different scale and for different reasons. We see that refugee crises demand the attention of volunteers, not only out in the field, but in the resettlement countries also. That's what I want to talk about now - what we can see and do in the United States.

Unfortunately, we're seeing in the U.S. a shift in public opinion away from the generally sympathetic attention of the American people to the problem of refugees to a sort of mistrust and indifference. Although they can't completely reverse the direction of this public apathy to refugees, I think that volunteers are capable of being a source of great support, and are needed to help stem this tide of public opinion. Peter Pond said something about the Khmer problem. The congressmen and senators have to hear from private people, not from hired flacks like me, or those whose viewpoints they already know. It must be said that we don't like the way the Khmer are being treated. It is up to us to be prepared to work on trouble spots and to provide the continued concern of the American public for refugees. We need our returned volunteers, the board members of refugees NGOs [non-governmental agencies], and concerned members of the voluntary organizations for what I call a "Refugee PAC", a refugee constituency that is not willing to see the traditional American role in humanitarian relief efforts and in welcoming to our country victims of oppression foregone. Refugee crises will continue and I believe that the U.S. must continue to carry out its tradition of humanitarian help. The flow of people in Indochina, Central America, Africa still requires our attention and concern, and this role of public education - of the volunteers participating in public education and refugee concern - is what we have to pay attention to now.

Let me give you a couple of agendas for your PAC. My items are very pragmatic, but they have been said in much more elegant fashion by Dale [DeHaan], Rick [Swartz] and others. They all have some relevance to our three years in Thailand.

The first part of the agenda deals with the Khmer. Even two and a half years after leaving Thailand, both Mort and I feel that this is a part of our lives that hasn't been brought to a close; that hasn't been handled well. We still have Khmer in the camps waiting to come to the U.S.

In 1979 more than a half a million came to the border of Thailand. The U.S. and other nations persuaded the Thai government to allow some of these Khmer to enter with the clear understanding that they would not remain permanently in Thailand. Now several hundred thousand Khmer have returned from the border to Cambodia, eight thousand have been resettled in various Western countries and forty to fifty thousand still remain in camps. Half of those in the camps still have some U.S. connections and their cases have been prepared for presentation to INS. We do have the numbers to allow those people to live here. They have no desire to return to Cambodia under any circumstances. This is the group that we must lobby to help. The U.S. government has found the stumbling block to be the interpretation by the INS officers of the regulations governing admissions. Whatever the merits of the INS case, a major problem is that the INS officers perceive that they have the backing of some elements of Congress and the U.S. public for their present course of action - which is to turn down these cases. The INS officers feel they can ignore the stated policy of the U.S. As individual citizens and groups we must let our representatives and the public know that this refusal to treat the remaining Khmer fairly and equitably does not represent our views. We have profound problems with the present situations which can be settled quickly with the public's help.

We must complete what we started out to do in 1979. This is an issue that I would put at the head of your agenda.

The next items on my agenda are ones that are close to my heart and so obvious that I am afraid even to raise them. But just in case I am in another refugee crisis I am going to say I spoke out. I was and am deeply disturbed by the lack of pre-planning for whatever the next refugee disaster may bring. As difficult as it is to anticipate when and where a new trouble spot will emerge, we should join together private, public and international agencies to think about resources, manpower needs and coordination.

I use the example of 1979 when, in that fall, the UNHCR and voluntary agencies already working in Thailand suddenly faced the task of trying to respond to the needs of several hundred thousand Khmer arriving on the Thai-Cambodian border. They arrived starving and in need of medical attention. Despite the fact that evidence of this eventuality was clear, and the UNHCR was certainly made aware of the evidence, neither they nor the ICRC nor the NGOs had a coordinated emergency program in place. In fact, the only thing that saved these laws was the coordination between the NGOs themselves. That had already been going on to take care of the Vietnamese and the Lao. Moreover, the decisions made in those first weeks of crisis are the decisions you live with for months, even if they are completely irrational.

The UNHCR does not have the capacity to prepare for sudden refugee crises because of policies and leadership and the way they are set up to operate. The UNHCR relies on the resources of various other private agencies to provide services to refugees. It does not have the capacity to prepare for prospective refugee disasters by organizing a disaster response team. The U.S. government, although very active in refugee assistance overseas and in relief assistance, does not have a coordinated crisis response mechanism for relief of refugee disaster. It has an AID office of disaster assistance which is very generous with money if you tell them what you want to use the money for. It can also bring other resources of the Defense Department and Civil Defense and provide tents and other equipment, but the office has no coordinating or planning function. It was set up to deal with natural disasters, not people disasters - not refugee disasters where politics are involved. The U.S. private voluntary organizations do some internal planning and preparation for crisis response, but they don't coordinate with each other. Rather, when the crisis occurs, the shotgun approach predominates with each agency sending its own assessment team to the crisis to determine needs, allocation of resources and where it will work, often deciding to put a team on the ground in places where they hadn't had teams before. Two countries have developed emergency response teams which coordinate the private and public efforts to dispatch the disaster teams to the fields - Sweden and Switzerland.

The UNHCR has encouraged the U.S. agencies to develop similar mechanisms. As far as I know, in the U.S. this activity hasn't taken place in a serious way, and if it has it has been very fragmented. There are tasks that need to be done by public and private agencies before we look at our next refugee flow. Individual citizens and volunteers can play a role in urging the private agencies to do this. Some of you are on the boards. You are the people that provide the money to the agencies.

Every crisis is different. The mix of the refugees is different. The regions are different. But I really believe that there are some problems that are the same. Some of the pre-planning tasks we could look at would be some identification and agreement by agencies on minimum standards of food, sanitation and medicine to be provided to a refugee in a crisis.

I don't want to sit around any more tables of the CCSDPT in whatever country I am, deciding whether a refugee should have 2 grams or 3 grams of rice. That is really awful to be doing in the middle of the crisis.

Regarding identification of each agency's capabilities in various regions, I think in a crisis those agencies which have been there before ought to be the ones to go in. They know the set up. Identification of agency expertise could be provided by assessment teams, as could identification of models for field coordination between government and private agencies and identification of an agency's capacities to utilize volunteers. I believe these are possible despite the region or the kinds of people involved.

Presently, our constituency, the advocates for refugees, is facing real political problems in Washington. The community faces challenges not only from INS, but also from the re-introduction of the Simpson-Mazzoli Bill and the Annual Refugee Number Review. Yet, the efforts to face these problems are fragmented, unfocused and, regrettably, in some cases naive. And always at the last minute. The inability of the voluntary agencies to sustain a joint Washington effort for information and liaison on refugee matters is really unfortunate. There have been ad hoc attempts recently to expand that with a joint-based effort and information gathering and strategy planning on refugee related legislation and executive developments. Our community, however, has been reluctant to continue any joint effort or implementation of this kind or give any ad hoc group a mandate for developing legislative strategies. There are some reasons for this reluctance.

First is the legitimate fear on the part of each individual agency that a joint effort might not represent interests of its own broader constituency. I do wish to point out, however, that times are changing and there are some issues on which we have to unite or we're going to face radical changes of the overall U.S. refugee policy. Moreover, many coalitions on all sorts of issues are formed successfully and without threatening the independence of each member. The second reason for the refusal to form a kind of action coalition is a bit more malicious and fairly widespread. It is that everybody wants to be his own Washington lobbyist, wants to develop his own contacts, to be his own mover and shaker. It is a very prevalent phenomenon among universities and business groups. And everyone likes to come to Washington. However, if a little of that moving and shaking is applied to a common goal, it is even better. People don't want to give up their contacts and their access. They don't want to share. That is why people don't join together when they are faced with a big legislative push. But I think the network of supporters of the agency can and does expect our best efforts and strategies to work on our mutual concerns.

My agenda has one final item: that of individual efforts with refugees - personal caseloads (like Simon Shargo had). I would like to make a modest plea for individual help in resettlement communities. We need to take on a few small cases. We need to help people find jobs. We need to help with language lessons. We need to help with school problems. We need to help find social security cards, look for medical care, etc. This takes a lot of personal help and sometimes the agencies don't have it. We also need to keep encouraging people to be sponsors.

In summary, there are things that volunteers can do. During a refugee crisis volunteers are essential for providing support, advocacy, education and protection of the refugee in the field. Volunteers who come to the field deserve our support and the intelligent attention of the receiving agencies. They deserve planning for their use and training. Volunteers, on the other hand, have an obligation to adhere to guidelines and modes of behavior outlined by the agencies and the host governments. Here at home the agenda for volunteer action is long and varied, but it is essential today that we work together on the problem of the Khmer, of consolidating our efforts in Washington to protect the interests of the refugee, and to consolidate and coordinate our pre-planning efforts for future refugee emergencies.

Thank you.

Peter Rose: I want to thank Sheppie for providing us with a number of bridges - a bridge from the past, from Simon Shargo's own experience with the holocaust, to the Abramowitz' experience with the genocide in

Cambodia, and the experience of many of you who were with that unfortunate series of incidents.

Sheppie also provided us with a bridge to tomorrow's discussion on improving services to refugees - hopefully at every level, including the voluntary level.

IMPROVING SERVICES FOR REFUGEES

Susan Forbes: I am Susan Forbes from the Refugee Policy Group. This session on "Improving Services for Refugees" is a very timely session. There is a good deal of discussion going on in Washington right now, as there is throughout the country and around the world, regarding the nature of services for refugees. I thought before the session began I would review what some of those initiatives are so that you'll have some context for hearing and then discussing the panelists' presentations.

The Refugee Act [of 1980] is up for reauthorization once more this year. I am sure you also know that the refugee program has been an evolving one. It is a program that has been under constant change and constant flux since its inception. As a matter of fact, there are many of us who feel that one of its major problems has been this very changing nature of the program.

There are several concrete proposals under serious consideration that form the context for our discussion. The administration has proposed in the 1984 budget to place all of the special refugee programs and assistance and service programs into block grants. This means that refugee cash assistance, refugee medical assistance, social services targeted assistance and the special funds that go to support school age children of refugees would be put into a single block grant, given to the state on a per-capita basis, using an allocation based on the number of time-eligible refugees within the state for the state to divide up and do as it pleases with that money. Obviously this gives quite a bit of discretion to the states in terms of developing a refugee program. That is part of the FY '84 budget. I am assuming that this will be the policy of the coming year. Of course, it must go to Congress and be discussed there, and it is not clear whether or not it will actually get Congressional approval or Congressional appropriations to implement the plan.

At the same time, a number of the federal agencies responsible for refugee affairs have been exploring whether other models of resettlement are feasible and would be desirable to implement. One of the changes being discovered would be the transfer of responsibility for cash assistance for refugees from state-administered programs to a voluntary agency model in which the resettlement agencies would be responsible for providing for all cash assistance and maintenance assistance for refugees during the first year in the country. There is also discussion about the possibilities of transferring the assistance program from being implemented through the AFDC [Aid to Families and Dependent Children], the general welfare program, to be administered by public agencies, but through a refugee specific program that would be designed to meet the special needs of refugees.

Also, there is considerable interest in different schemes for case load management, for refugee services, for mechanisms to provide for more coordination between the cash and medical assistance on the one side and social services on the other.

Other issues being discussed are ones concerning the timing of services, what the appropriate sequence is. Most of you have heard some discussion about "front-end loading" as opposed to other strategies for providing services. That is again under review. We are also talking about the possibilities for developing funding for consortiums of service providers rather than individual service providers.

Most of us familiar with the refugee program know that whatever the national policies or the state policies are for refugees, those policies will only be as good as their implementation on the local level.

This panel will be discussing some suggestions about various problems with the programs and some points about strengths of the program in the local areas and strategies at that local area for improving services.

Our first speaker will be Monsignor Bryan Walsh, who is President of Catholic Community Services, Inc., the south Florida affiliate of the U.S Catholic Conference on Migration and Refugee Services. CCS is a multi-functional social services agency with a $19 million budget. It serves 8 countries with 54 service outlets. Monsignor Walsh is also Vice President of the National Conference of Catholic Charities and a board member of the Child Welfare League of America, as well as a member of the Council on Accreditation. He has worked with refugees since 1955 and so brings to this issue a wealth of experience and information.

Msgr. Bryan Walsh: When I talk about refugees I always like to start with a story about a refugee cat who came from Cuba in the Mariel sealift in 1980. This cat experienced what the 125,000 Marielitos had - namely, that for the first time in 20 years, the government decided not to give any financial assistance. This cat was in the part of Miami where Cuban refugees are settled, called "Little Havana" by the Anglos. It is located in the southwest area of Miami, so the Cubans called it "La Sowesera". The cat was hungry and was trying to figure out a way to survive when it discovered a hole in the wall. Inside that hole was a mouse. The mouse had survived a long time in Little Havana, so it was sort of a stand-off. The cat sat down and started thinking: how am I going to cope with this.

Deciding on a strategy, it went around the corner and started barking like a dog. Everyone knows that a dog and a cat don't stay in the same place, so the mouse figured the coast was clear and came out. The cat pounced on the mouse and had his first lunch in exile. The moral of the story is, if you are going to eat in exile, you'd better talk two languages.

I also think there is another moral to the story: despite what we all do in the area of resettlement, the ultimate *sine qua non* is the resourcefulness of the individual who would be resettled. I am absolutely convinced that the success of the Cuban phenomenon in Miami, which has been written up in everything from *Fortune* magazine on down, is due (at least 75% I sometimes say) to the resourcefulness of the indigenous Cuban community as it grew, and the other 25 percent can be attributed to the intervention of ourselves and the federal government. However, in my more cynical moments I think the success was despite our intervention in the process. Our intervention was not always in the best interests.

The U.S. resettlement system has been characterized as a highly decentralized set of public and private arrangements that vary widely by locality and certainly vary widely not only from year to year, but sometimes from month to month. The situation becomes even more confusing when we realize that there is no real convening process, much less any real direction - there is no bottom line where you say this person is responsible, "the buck stops here". During the Mariel crisis, when we finally got the federal government to send somebody to Miami, I asked him, "Are you in charge?". He said, "No, no, no. I just came down here to help." I said, "Well please go back to Washington and tell them to send somebody in charge", because it is a federal responsibility. The local community and the state as well as the local voluntary agencies have no control over immigration. We have no control over which refugees come in, which refugees don't.

It is a federal responsibility that was decided by the Supreme Court. The federal government must, by law and in every other way, be held accountable for whatever happens to the refugees who are in our midst as a result of its policy - or lack of policy.

After 27 years, I tend to look at the whole issue from the perspective of a local provider of services. I have been through it all since the days of the Hungarian Freedom Fighters. In those days, the local, state and city governments had no idea there was any such thing as a refugee, they were not even conscious of it - and the federal government's responsibility, like the volags', was ended at the Port of Entry. Once people were in this country it was an entirely voluntary process. I can claim some role in changing that, with regard to the Cubans in 1960, and getting the federal government to assume responsibility for support and resettlement throughout the country. We have seen the various other changes that have since occurred. State and city governments became involved in about 1965, and then the free-for-all started in 1980 with the Mariel crisis when we saw all kinds of other actors come on to the scene.

I have two areas I would like to briefly raise for consideration. For a couple of years I have chaired the Council on Accreditation, a task force on the accreditation of agencies which serve refugees in the resettlement process at the local level. I think that outside of local agencies, which are credited by the Council, very few people even know of the existence of the standards. I call them to your attention because of the discussion concerning professionalization yesterday. The Council on Accreditation is sponsored by the National Conference of Catholic Charities, the National Jewish Agencies, the Lutherans, the Child Welfare League of America, and the Family Service Association which came together a number of years ago to develop standards and provisions for the accreditation of all kinds of services in the social [work] field. We have now gone through the resettlement process and it was a tremendous experience in clarifying our own thinking about who was responsible for what, and what the real standards of the provisions should be.

The other areas that I want to mention is the cracks in the surface of what is happening. We have identified about five thousand people in our community who have applications pending for political asylum. However, the discretionary power which is given to the local district of INS to grant work permits has been abused. This power has been arbitrarily used to deny work permits pending the results of the adjudication of the petitions. One day we go to INS and get work permits, the next day, with the same kind of people, we don't get work permits.

The INS director has the authority, on humanitarian grounds, to give work permits just as he has the authority to release people from detention. But it is a game that is going on, and it seems to be directed at shutting up advocates. They tell us that if you're going to advocate for these people you had better put your money where your mouth is, and, therefore, it is up to you to support them - you brought them here. We are the villains. We created the problems, and therefore we should pay the bill. I am sure this is not only with the local INS director, but is also coming from higher up and the local director thinks he is responding to what the administration and the federal bureaucracy wants at the present time. However, the logic of what is going on in Washington is beyond my comprehension.

The situation has gotten very serious. We see constant abuse of the U.S. law, as well as international law, by our government. This leads to what is happening in other parts of the country with regard to Salvadorians. Where do we take a stand as social advocates in order to help people? This is what we are faced with when we go out to help people in the local community.

Then there is the question of church sanctuary. Milwaukee has done it; Seattle has done it. Other churches all the way to Arizona have done it, and we are faced with this at the present time. Frankly, I have told the Archbishop that I expect more churches to be on the spot in this regard. What does church sanctuary mean? It is a form of protest. It is not a confrontation. It is not a defiance of U.S. law. Rather, it is a way of gaining some form of respite in which we can cause people to reflect on the fact that there are inadequacies in our laws for carrying out the national purpose of caring for refugees; calling attention to the fact that the government is breaking the law as it exists at the present time.

Susan Forbes: Our next speaker is David Pierce, who is an expert on immigration policy and has been a Foreign Service Officer working on refugee matters during the Ford, Carter and Reagan administrations. He is currently on loan from the U.S. Foreign Service to consortiums in cities in Orange County, California. It is his experience with Orange County's refugee program that he'll be speaking about today.

David Pierce: Thank you. I am going to put on my local and state government hat for a minute. This is where I have been recently. I am sort of the new kid on the block in this area, but I have been interested in immigration and flows for a long time. Obviously that includes refugees.

I am very happy to have had the chance to work in a dynamic, changing area like Orange County, which does not have very many Cubans but has a lot of Indochinese. I would like to talk about public-private sector cooperation in the context of recognizing that even the arrival of one immigrant, one refugee imposes adjustment costs that are significant. Most of those costs - and I am talking about time and attention as well as money and resources - are borne by the refugee himself or herself. However, some of those costs are borne by the community in which the refugee settles or stays. They are real and they are significant. They don't necessarily lead to problems, but they are there and we need to recognize that. If I had to summarize what I would say in terms of facilitating private and public sector cooperation in this resettlement process - and by extension to other immigrants as well - it is that virtually everyone involved in the process needs to look all the time for common interests, common objectives and common experiences. Not only among the refugee resettlement community itself, but within the institutions that are even peripheral to resettlement, within the community at large.

Local governments - counties, school districts, cities - must be involved with refugees. In California local governments have some direct responsibility to the adjustment process that refugees are going through. Here the counties generally handle health and welfare, the school districts handle education, and the cities generally handle public safety services, housing, etc. What the local governments have in common is that they are all, in some way, responsible for the definition of the community. In counseling terms, they are the mirror - the politicians and the appointed officials - for the community. They are the ones who reflect to the community its sense of well-being, its sense of stress, its sense of threat. Even if you don't think the cities or the counties or the states or anybody else provide any services at all, and even if they don't they are not totally peripheral to the process, they are not peripheral to the definition of community. For this reason it is worth paying attention to them.

The environment in which the constituencies are served means a lot as to whether the flows of people who are coming in are greeted with openness or hostility. And the larger the flows of refugees the more important it is to pay attention to that fact. To illustrate, a recent headline read "New Orleans Seeks To Halt New Cuban Refugee Project". Apparently what happened was that a YMCA in New Orleans made a proposal to resettle 125 Cubans in their building and in their area, to find them jobs, and so on. It was an integrated, sensible and reasonable program from the point of view of resettlement. City officials had no idea this was coming. They found out about it indirectly - and they were surprised. Now, the last thing you want to do to any bureaucracy, is to surprise people with the unanticipated, the unexpected.

We can all handle change. Indeed, our country is organized around the principle of continuous, ever rapid change; our whole economy is structured that way. But we are, at heart, a socially cautious people. We don't like to see unexpected change. We have difficulty dealing with it. Yet the issues of community tensions and concern often revolve around precisely that - an unexpected change. All of a sudden 125,000 people we didn't expect or know what to do with are in our midst and that is scary. There are many things that can be done to reduce that fear. Much of the fear, which may be expressed in racial, ethnic or other terms, turns out at its roots to be future shock, a fear of the unknown.

City officials, county officials and others can help by sharing with their constituencies what they think is likely to happen, what kinds of changes are in the wind, whether they think there are going to be proposals for new programs, whether they think flows of secondary migrants are coming and what they are trying to do about it. It gives them a sense of predictability and, in turn, control. It is not total control, none of us have total control, but it takes the edge off the scare. It is less frightening if you know or if you think that you are in touch with the people who are anticipating problems and that somebody is working on them. Then, when people hear about it, their first reaction is "Yes, I heard this is coming" or "I heard something about it" and "Somebody is working on it". That is a very important channel to set up.

We see that in bold relief in looking at what happened with the Indochinese who came in '75, and again with the secondary migrants and the newcomers in '79. You don't have to be an official; you don't have to have a title. As a consortium city's foreign service officer nobody really knew who I was or what I was doing. I had no formal or informal authority to do anything. You don't have to have authority; you have to make communication linkages, to sit down and talk, to share the sense of what is happening with people so they are not as surprised, to give them what they need to deal with this sense of unease and help them to be able to say to the community, "It's okay to feel bothered by this rapid change". We all are bothered by things that we can't totally predict and control, but it is the American experience, it is the American way. We are all immigrants.

Having focused on local governments, I am going to take a look at the fourth estate - the media, the press. Some of you may know the flagship of the freedom chain of newspapers, *The Orange County Register.* It is a rather famous or infamous - depending on your point of view- newspaper. Its position is that any kind of government, any kind of public anything, is immoral because it survives on taxes that are extracted by force from taxpayers - the only legitimate public function is that to which we would contribute voluntarily. They ideologically tend to believe that everybody, were it not for government, would be able, hard working and would hustle the meanest, lowest, grubbiest and nastiest jobs in an effort to move ahead and work in society. So, you can count on them, editorially and in their stories, to ascribe these "Horatio Alger" work ethic kinds of behavior patterns to everybody across the board, including refugees. That is a very powerful device if you can tap into it and use it, if you can help to communicate the view that these people are okay. However, you are going to have to live with the negative side of it, and I suggest that every newspaper, every media outlet, every fourth estate operation is going to have a mixed bag of these things.

Let me suggest, too, that you not neglect other ethnic groups - the blacks, the Hispanics, the others who are affected, too, by the presence of new refugees. It is important that we recognize that they are bothered by unpredictable change.

Two other things - a couple of models for private-public cooperation from the experience that I have seen in Orange County. First is a model of local determination, of creatively using social service dollars bringing in not only the public sector and the private voluntary sector, but also the private-profit sector. Some of the interest from the profit-sector revolves around labor shortages, the scarcity of people at entry level positions. In fact, what often seems like a problem when you first look at it - overcrowded housing, the large extended family crowded into a house that was built for a single family unit - may be redefined. To the profit sector there are, say, four or five wage earners in one house.

Let me also suggest the model of reception, placement and integration into the American work situation and experience that looks something like a reverse Peace Corps model. This is what we are moving toward. Maybe I am biased because I am an ex-Peace Corps volunteer and I remember what it was like going from another culture through a transition training camp kind of arrangement into a new one. We didn't learn enough to speak the language well, but we did learn enough to start learning and to feel comfortable with learning. It was the same with job skills. We didn't know enough in the training camp that we could function effectively in the environment once we got there. So we moved in to what amounted to a sheltered or protected environment where people understood that we were going to have trouble for a couple of months while we were learning how to work in that bureaucratic and work environment. Having people go through refugee processing centers for 24 weeks of English and cultural orientation looks a lot like the Peace Corps training I went through the other way, going east instead of west. What is missing in that model is what happens when they get here - the decentralized structure that Msgr. Walsh talked about. I think what is needed is a work-fare kind of a program, two or three days of actual work experience on the job, beginning almost the minute the refugees arrive. They would learn how to work and spend the other two or three days a week in concentrated efforts to put a theoretical side to that. "What happened yesterday when the boss got mad? Why did he get mad?", that sort of thing.

A question raised earlier was how long does it take for folks to be job ready, to find a job and work effectively in our situation? The model that is thrown around in career placement and in counseling and in books like *What Color is Your Parachute?* is that for every thousand dollars of income a year you expect, it is going to take a week to find that job. That is for people who are already working, who have a work history in this country, who speak the language, who understand the bureaucratic structures of how to work and how to look for a job. If you are talking about a minimum wage job, which is something on the order of $7,000 gross, you're talking about 7-8 weeks minimum just to find the job. Add on how long it takes you to catch up from zero to the skills we all carry around with us - how to work in this situation, how to look for work, how to establish that relationship, how to speak the language adequately for employment.

Let me close on this note. We recently had stories in the Orange County newspaper that said there was a rush to welfare by refugees who were moving on to the general relief program and away from the RCA because of the rule changes. The implication was that there was a huge rise in the number of people receiving assistance. With some help from the county, we got a retraction and we got out the story that the dependency rate is dropping, and is accelerating in its drop.

Susan Forbes: Thank you David. Our next speaker will be Pat Waltermire who is a native of Colorado, a graduate of the University of Colorado, who then spent 17 years in Idaho with the United Presbyterian Church. Pat moved to California in 1973 and continued to be active in church groups, especially on issues of social justice. Past Chair of the San Francisco Refugee Forum, she is currently Program Director of the Ecumenical Refugee Resettlement and Sponsorship Services in Northern California and Nevada.

Pat Waltermire: Thank you Susan. One of the advantages of being part of the last panel is that you get to reflect on some of the questions that have come up before. One of the things that intrigued me most about a previous presentation was the question, "Do models serve for all ethnic groups?" Church World Service, which began in 1946, has worked across the board with each ethnic group. Currently, we are resettling 30 ethnic groups from 26 different nationalities. That is a broad spectrum. Many of those people have come to the northern California-Nevada area. Hence, we have a bit of experience with most. "Does the same model work for each ethnic group?" No, it does not.

Experience, job readiness, all of these are different. Hence, you have to tailor what you do to the group with whom you are working at a given point in time. We tend to lump people together in the U.S. In fact, when I first met Susan she was in San Francisco talking about some of the problems that are being discussed in Washington. One of the terms she used, which I found almost frightening because of its degradation, was the term, "the undigested lump". I think that when you think about that particular term it raises very interesting reactions in all of us.

I want to talk about serving that "undigested lump" at this point, and to reflect something that Michael Friedline said.

Church World Service has always used the congregational model of resettlement, although there are variations on that theme within Church World Service as well as within the 14 denominations of CSW. We adhere to that principle as being the best and most effective, although perhaps not the most efficient from the time aspect. There are several parallels between the refugee situation of people and the immigrant situation. If we reflect on the history of the U.S. and all the ethnic groups from which we may have come, we see a commonality - that of the first experience of coming into a new culture (even though you might have been English speaking) and the tendency of all of us to associate with those with whom we feel comfortable. Hence, the self-ghettoization of America is something that is a very rich part of our past, and still is seen in many of the large cities. San Francisco is one of those: New York is another; so are Baltimore and Boston. These are areas where there are rich ethnic cultural groups grouped together. One of the drawbacks of that kind of ghettoization is a lack of touch with the American culture *per se,* the American culture which is rich because it is enriched by all of those ethnic groups.

One of the advantages to a congregational model sponsorship is that of direct contact with the American culture in the shelter of the community - a sheltered situation where you can learn, make mistakes, and not be castigated for those mistakes. Obviously it is time consuming and it is resource consuming, but the voluntary sector is not as concerned about the consuming of time as is the sector where people are paid for their time. And it does work. But it is slower and there is no way in the waves of people that have had to be resettled in the last eight years in the U.S. that this kind of model could be utilized for all. However, it can be used in various ways as a model.

We have heard the term 'time expiration'. We talk about 'time expired' refugees. Refugee resettlement projects also time expire. We are in the midst of one of those time expirations. The particular project which I head will go out of existence at the end of May 1984. As a part of that phase-down we have been meeting in 23 cities in northern California and Nevada with persons from the private sector who have been involved in sponsorship or have been involved in service to refugees. What we are doing in those meetings is a community by community needs assessment. We hear about Orange County, Los Angeles and San Diego, but northern California is pretty well inundated with refugees as well. It is estimated that they may be forty percent of the secondary migration. When you say forty percent secondary migration you rarely even think about out migrations, although I am sure it is not quite that high. However, there are significant movements of Hmong into the Central Valley of California. In Merced, a town of 20,000 persons, there are now at least 5,000 Hmong. That is a heavy inundation. Areas such as Fresno, Merced, Stockton and Sacramento all have had significant movements of the Hmong people. Their reasons for coming are beginning to be clear. They have found, over the years they have been in the U.S., that their skills are not applicable to our industrialized society. Hence, they have felt that they can and will return to using that talent which they had in their home country: agriculture. Hence, they are moving back to an area where they use the expertise which they have.

One problem with this is a problem common to all farmers. When one farmer makes a big profit on a crop, the next year everybody plants that crop. The Hmong tend to have that same strand of human nature. In the Central Valley where they have resettled there are acres of cherry tomatoes rotting on the vines because the price has dropped and they are unmarketable. With a little help in planning, this can be changed. We are trying to interest the local community to support this kind of an initiative on the part of the refugees.

The church community is by far the most organized of all volunteer groups. But they also 'plug in' to many other voluntary areas: service clubs, social clubs, all of places where volunteer service is utilized in the community.

By doing a needs assessment of the refugees within a community we do several things. First, we raise the awareness of the fact that refugees are a part of the community with needs but also with contributions to give. We also put in perspective the things that need to be assumed by government or by its agencies.

There are many things that can be done on a voluntary basis: job banks, tutoring, ESL classes, training in interview techniques, all of those things that not only can be applied to the refugee population, but that can also include, perhaps, the undocumented and those in need who are not the refugee community. It is in drawing those parallels that some of the backlash that is focused on the newcomers can be diffused. What is needed is a coordinating body that can keep that going. This is one need that we have not yet been able to fulfill.

Refugees are not a people to be set apart, but should be seen first as those in need and then in terms of the tremendous contributions they can make to our society.

Susan Forbes: Our last speaker will be Richard Brown, a former Foreign Service Officer who served in three posts in Southeast Asia in the early 1960s, and later in the Middle East and in Africa. Refugee resettlement or social services is a family business or family interest. His wife is the Coordinator of Western Massachusetts Cambodian Foster Children program. He is involved in the program known as 'cluster resettlement' coordinated through the Lutheran Social Services.

Richard Brown: Thank you. I am relatively new to refugee resettlement work, compared to many of the other participants in this conference. I have another perspective, also, in that I work on a somewhat smaller scale in western New England than most of the participants. I also have the advantage of being new enough that I haven't yet learned what can't be done. I have been able to try with my colleagues some innovative efforts to draw upon that very volunteerism that Sheppie Abramowitz extolled.

I did get off to a start with refugees twenty-two years ago in the foreign service in Hong Kong as a visa officer interviewing Chinese refugees, and managed to resist the tide of nay sayers and help some of the flotsam of the Oriental Exclusion Act [Chinese Exclusion Act] - elderly ladies who had been left behind and who had been rejected by generations of visa officers - join their families. That was a very satisfying human service. It left in me a sense that this is the kind of service in which I wanted to work. Later, the more abstract work of the foreign service career was not quite as satisfying, so I was quite ready - especially since I had seen in Hong Kong just how cruelly indifferent some bureaucrats can be when they have the lives of the powerless in their hands - to join the ranks when Peter Pond came to Amherst and told us about the Cambodian refugee crisis.

I was horrified to hear about the indifference, the cruelty that had been practiced by the representatives of this country in the refugee selection process in the camps in Thailand. I was also horrified to learn more about what Cambodians had been through, and to realize that in western New England we had really done relatively little to help in this great mission. So, I joined first as a sponsor to help organize a cluster of refugee families in Amherst. Again, this is a small scale, a small town - we have about 70 Cambodian refugees, 10 families and 12 foster children - but it works in New England. I then joined Peter Pond and his staff in the Lutheran Service Association to work in New England at helping to establish other clusters. This was the model we chose because we had a particular kind of situation in western New England, not big urban areas, not much professional infrastructure that could provide services, not a pattern of having services provided to the substratum as you find in big city areas. However, we did have certain strengths. We had compassionate people; we had churches and synagogues that could be enlisted in a cause when they were informed of the crisis. They could be mobilized to help provide a kind of link to inspire the communities themselves through networking and through public information on a small scale and to provide services to the refugees as they came in.

We and the Lutheran Service Association are not essentially service providers. What we try to do with the refugee families is to find, inspire and list organized clusters of sponsors. The clusters of sponsors in turn bring, in time, clusters of families which are able to provide a kind of neutral re-inforcement. I am sure this is not new to many of you. However, we are talking here about a small scale, we are talking about even small villages, small churches of about 100 members who join, who are "empowered" to use Peter Pond's term, to find the indigenous leadership in the community, within the churches, within the community service clubs or wherever, and inspire them, empower them, to take on this new mission, this mission which is not only to Cambodians, but to any who are homeless.

Because it has to start somewhere we began with the most immediate crisis, that of the Cambodian refugees, people who have no place to go. They can't go back to Cambodia. They fear the persecution they will experience if they are forced back to those border areas. They certainly cannot stay in Thailand. The towns and small cities of New England have responded and I think they will continue to respond because the sponsors have educated themselves and each other about the crisis, about Cambodians, about refugees, so they are able to provide services or to inspire the community to provide services that the refugees need. And they are able to inspire other sponsors as well. We have seen this happen. We have seen that the refugees have done much better in terms of reaching self-sufficiency than in some of the heavily impacted places like Boston and Providence. In areas of western New England where we have sponsors that have provided this continual link with the community and with each other resettlement has been much more dramatic and positive. There are clusters less than a year old in New England where every family is reasonably self-sufficient - fully employed, off welfare, perhaps still receiving some food stamp aid, but otherwise relying on their own work and jobs and some vocational advice from sponsors.

The cluster resettlement approach has been far more effective than any advocacy by people involved professionally with refugees. Those involved in what some call "a mission of advocacy" have helped to organize trips to Thailand to see for themselves the situation of the refugees in the camps and to bring back to their communities the story with slides and lectures. They are organizing vigils and public worship services. The kind of broad wholistic mission that they are undertaking is putting a kind of 'new blood' into the Cambodian or refugee resettlement issue that Sheppie Abramowitz was saying is generally needed.

Susan Forbes: Thank you. We will now turn to our discussant to make some comments about the presentation, and since he has promised to keep his remarks brief we should have time afterwards for questions and comments from the audience. It is a particular pleasure for me to introduce Gary Rubin.

Gary describes himself as an historian and specialist in immigration matters. He has recently moved from the Institute of Human Relations at the American Jewish Committee to become Director of Planning at the American Council of Nationalities Services. There he has been involved with a number of different projects including some demonstration projects that ACNS has been implementing in three different communities on case management services.

IMPROVING SERVICES FOR REFUGEES

Gary Rubin: I would like, in the role of the discussant, to engage with Richard Brown, Pat Waltermire, Sheppie Abramowitz and Peter Pond in some reconsideration of the volunteer-professional relationship. Specifically, I would like to say some good things about professionalism, a perspective which may have been overlooked in some of the discussions. In doing so I don't want to be seen as saying anything negative about the presentations concerning volunteerism, which I fully support. I particularly think that the kinds of organized volunteer services discussed by Richard Brown and by Pat Waltermire are extremely important, but I also think that it is equally important to carefully consider the gains of professionalism in the field and to try to reach some balance - not dichotomy, but balance - between professionalism and volunteerism. There are three specific points about professionalism.

The first is that it's often different to sit in a room with a number of refugee advocates and discuss the refugee field than to go out into the political world - the world outside this room - and argue about refugees with people who know little or nothing about them, but who will decide the course of the refugee programs in this country. The refugee program in terms of funding and in terms of orientation is now very much in the hands of Congress, in the hands of the administration, of people who see the world from a very different perspective than the way we do. If we are going to be successful, we have to address that audience in terms they understand, in terms they can respond to, and in terms they think are important. What is important in refugee resettlement at the federal level - and probably some state levels - is not compassion, it's not enthusiasm, it's not inspiration. What's important is tracking, and monitoring, and reducing welfare rolls. The fact is - no matter how we think about it among ourselves - unless we can address them with what are essentially budgetary concerns we will find the refugee program continuing to be cut, as it was cut last year and as it's threatened to be cut in the future. What we have to do is to be able to address them by saying that the refugee world is becoming increasingly professionalized, that we are able to do language training and job training better, that we will be able to reduce the welfare rolls, because if we don't the result will be fewer refugees in this country and less money to give services to refugees. Therefore, if we want to attain our main goal - which is service to refugees - we had better be able to address them in terms that are of concern to them.

Secondly, having just talked about the necessity [to become more professional], I also want to say something about its desirability. It is a very difficult thing to resettle refugees. If you listened to any of the presentations, one thing kept coming across. Language training is not easy. Job training is not easy. Such programs require, on the part of the person dealing with the refugee, a knowledge of the theory of the subject, a training in the subject, experience in the subject, supervision. It requires, in other words, a certain amount of professionalism. While we need volunteerism, we will not do effective resettlement without that training in theory and supervision which can only happen with a professional orientation. While I am not attacking - and I want to make that clear - the notion of voluntarism, I would like to say that if we do have a negative attitude towards professionalism we will do worse resettlement and that is not what we need now.

Thirdly, I have a negative reaction to what sometimes is implied, although not always stated, in these discussions; that is, that what you gain and what you can gain only by going to the volunteer section is 'compassion and enthusiasm and inspiration', I have seen those qualities in the professional ranks and I think it is a real mistake to say that the professional workers cannot be enthusiastic, that they cannot be inspirational, that they cannot be compassionate. The real task is not making a dichotomy between the 'cold professional' and the 'compassionate volunteers', but joining together in a compassionate coalition.

I also want to make a couple of comments about David Pierce's very good presentation. Again, I am not arguing with him, but amplifying some of the points and asking some questions about how we proceed on it.

David talked about the costs of refugee resettlement and the costs to communities. I would suggest that instead of using the term "cost", he use the term "investment". Pat Waltermire was absolutely right in saying that if you look not only at the long term, but also at the middle term, refugees are an asset to the community. We may have to pay for them in the beginning, but eventually, as all the research shows, they contribute considerably to the community. The people here from Miami with the 20 years Cuban experience, from northern California, from southern California, from western Massachusetts have testified to that fact. "Cost" doesn't seem to be the word that captures the refugee experience. "Investment" does and I would suggest more use of that kind of term. Yes, we have to lay out money, but we lay it out for future gains.

I also ask a question about David's final point, having to do with getting a job quickly no matter what kind of job because it gives some work experience. I would raise a question about this point for the consideration of people in the refugee field as to whether we have sufficiently studied what the economists are saying in terms of the work experience in the United States. What is said in the refugee field is that any kind of work is work and there's a ladder that goes from the lowest kind of work to the highest kind of work. Thus, as long as we get people a job, they are already on a stream in which they can be socially mobile and wind up very successful. Some economists are questioning that assumption.

If you look at some of the literature about the experience of the black community and the job market for example, there are two labor markets in the United States: a primary sector - which is what essentially we would call 'good' jobs, professional jobs - and a secondary sector - the insecure, low-paying jobs. There is increasing dichotomy between the primary and secondary sectors. Real questions are raised about whether a person in a secondary sector has a chance to move into the primary sector. We in the refugee field would have to ask questions about the assumptions of whether getting the first unskilled job really puts somebody on the track of upward mobility. If you look at it in terms of investment, might not there be a better pay-off from the society at large as well as from the point of view of the refugees to invest a little more in training so the person can enter the primary labor market, therefore accruing greater gains not only to himself or to herself, but also to society at large.

My final point is this: how successful we are in settling refugees has a direct impact on our refugee policy and on our refugee intake. If what we spoke of earlier is being generous in terms of policy, in terms of accepting people to this country, then there will be no more powerful instrument in arguing for generousity than to point out that people who come here are successful in contributing to the society. What we are dealing with here is not just a social service question. As important as that is, it is also important that the entire refugee system - intake policy, attitude toward world crises, attitude towards first asylum - will be very much shaped by the kinds of questions we dealt with at this session, namely how good are we at working with refugees?

Thank you.

Susan Forbes: I'd like to know if any of the panelists would like to respond to Gary's comments or each other's comments. David?

David Pierce: Two very quick comments. First, the term "investment" is something we've been using for the year and a half that I have been in Orange County, California. Generally, we tend to put in terms of short-run, or immediate cost-of-the-adjustment-process, and long-run adjustment. I agree that investment is a critical concept to put in front of people. I think it is important to keep highlighting, where possible, the evidence that investment is in fact paying off.

The second comment I would make is that I don't think we have to try to re-create everyone's experience. Virtually everyone in this room, I suspect, has gone through several initial jobs, initial contacts with what is nicely called 'the world of work' in the U.S. to get to the situation that you are in now. In every one of those jobs you learn something about how to work, you learn about bureaucracy. I feel that accessing the primary sector is less and less a function of skin-color or ethnicity than it is a function of some very specific skills that need to be picked up early regarding how you work in this country, how you work in the primary sector. Internships are a way to begin. There has been a proliferation of internship programs that are doing precisely the same thing. The best ones combine work experience where risks and learning can take place with feed-back mechanisms from people who have already made the transition into the primary sector. This generally takes place in technical fields, but it could be effective in more general fields as well. It is not "get them in a job and get them off the dole" that I am suggesting. It is, rather, recognize that you are talking about a whole series of complex skills that are going to take time and attention to learn.

One other comment: there are political limits on how special we can make our programs for refugees. One of the attractive points of using a work-fair program [work in exchange for support payments] is that while it is perceived by the public at large as a negative not a positive, when looked at carefully, it turns out to be a positive. It ought to be sold and implemented on the principle that this is a pilot program to do welfare and public assistance in a better way, a way to integrate, to help refugees get the kinds of skills that they need to be competitive in the primary sector.

Person in audience (unidentified): I agree that we must have professionals to guide and to advise clusters of sponsors, ecumenical groups working with refugees, and I hope that we have been doing that successfully in New England. But I think it would be a mistake to fail to introduce to those areas of our country where professional refugee resettlement people are not in abundant supply the experience of refugee resettlement. It is essential that if we are to build this 'new blood', this new national consensus on "what we should be doing about refugees in the world", it is important for the communities of our country to make this issue their own. I think the best way they can do that is to have the experience through their own community.

Susan Forbes: There are a number of innovative programs around the country which are trying to do exactly that, particularly programs in which employment services and English language training are integrated within the same setting, and where job developers and job placement counselors are actually teaching parts of the English language training so that the refugees have the exposure to both sides of the equation and are able to see the relationship between learning the language and learning job skills.

Robert DeVecchi [from the floor]: Is the word "professionalism" a buzz word for federal dollars? Is it a cover word for saying that refugee resettlement should be a federal responsibility, and in looking at the balance sheets?

Gary Rubin: Bob, you could probably answer the question better than I. After the session I am going to put that one to you, but I'll try to say a couple of things about it.

If you took an untrained individual, gave him or her two months of training and said you are going to put that person in the primary job sector you would be naive. We must remember that a number of refugees come to the U.S. with skills. The two months of training is not going to teach the only skills they need to know in order to get into the primary or the secondary job markets. It is more of a question of transition and, possibly, adding a little training than it is of training people from the beginning. When people with that kind of background come to the U.S. and are urged to go into secondary labor market jobs, it is not only a very difficult transition for them to make (I sometimes think of what would happen if I went to another country and somebody told me to go into one of those jobs; how I would react), but it also doesn't make sense from the point of view of society at large because those people will be less of an economic asset to all of us if they are not able to take advantage of skills they brought with them. Also, I think that it is a mistake, not only in the refugee field but in the immigration field in general, to see the issue as every job that an immigrant or refugee accepts takes away a job from an American, or that any job that is occupied by an American is a job that is not going to be occupied by an immigrant or refugee. A person who is employed spends, and a person who is employed acts in the economy and creates demand. People who are working create jobs as well as occupying a job that somebody else doesn't have. And the higher up they are in the economic structure, the more that is true. In other words if we take an investment attitude and say that a person who could operate at a higher level with a little more training ought to get that, this would have positive economic ripple effects on the larger society, including job demand.

On the second point: obviously, the more professional a person, the more it's going to cost. The better your workers, the more they are going to demand and the more they are going to deserve. It is my conviction that when I use "professional", I am not using it as a buzz word to get money, I am using it because I have a conviction that professional resettlement work in cooperation with the volunteer sector produces better results than non-professional resettlement work. I think that we ought to be professional in all kinds of things, including professional outreach.

In our agency we have just hired a professional direct-mail specialist to raise money from the general public. This is necessary not only because it raises money, but because the general public is better informed about what we do, creating a broad base of support. So, when I say "become professional" I mean become professional in all kinds of ways, including reaching out. We have to be professional in outreach services as well as resettlement services.

RETROSPECT AND PROSPECT

PETER ROSE: This morning I received a letter which said, "Dear Peter, I wish you had not sent me the final program of the Conference which takes place as this letter arrives. Unfortunately, I have a meeting that meets as a full board only once every two months and the fact that I simply could not miss that obligation is the only thing which softens my disappointment at not being with you. There are so many friends and colleagues who are on the program that I miss the fraternal pleasure almost as much as I do the superbly planned conference itself." It was signed "Leo Cherne".

Leo's letter prompts me to say a few words about planning the conference.

Barry Stein wondered if this whole conference was an elaborate plan to bring my friends together to meet my other friends as well as to honor the memory of Simon Shargo. In a very real sense, it was. As some of you know, for the last few years I have been trying to get a fix on refugee policy, to get into the network of refugee services, to learn the lingo of the club, to know about "ICMs", "VOLAGS", "Refcords", "MAAs", "service providers", and all those things to try to figure out how the system works and where it breaks down to understand the debates from the highest levels of government and the United Nations to the protectors, assisters, movers, shakers, sponsors and advocates - as Sheppie called them.

My own research has taken me all over the country, to Geneva, Vienna, Rome, Tel Aviv and all over Southeast Asia - in cities and the refugee camps. Many of you have been there, too, and for far longer periods than I. In those places I interviewed and watched a number of people interact with their colleagues and with the refugees. In many cases I had the experience of going into the camps or into the offices and having people expect me to begin asking them about the refugees themselves - "How many are there?" "How are they doing?" and so forth - because that is what people ask. And I would say, "Yes, I am interested

RETROSPECT AND PROSPECT

in that, but I want to know what you do". They'd said, "Me?" and I'd say, "Yes, you". Then we would start what became a very informal and often a very long interview - and in some cases a very long relationship.

In each place I spoke to a number of people - altogether, hundreds. I thought that someday I'd like to reciprocate their generosity, their hospitality, to bring them here and, as Barry said, to have them meet each other as well as my colleagues and my students. That is how many of those on the program came to be invited to join us here. Among them are several of my former students still actively involved in refugee work themselves. Many of you have met two of them Eve Burton and Margaret Chamberlain - who will be on the platform soon. Before I turn things over to Margaret, I want to tell you about something that happened last night at our home.

Vann is a recent arrival to Northampton, a refugee from Vietnam by way of Songklah who Eve Burton sponsored along with two others. When Vann came to the house last night, she asked Eve and me about all the people who were there, "What are they doing here?" It was very difficult to explain to her that they (you) all work with refugees. I was tempted to tell her that you were the reason that she was here in the U.S. But of course that would have been wrong. As Eve explained to her in Vietnamese, she was the reason that we are here, all of us. She is the reason we do what we do.

All the links of the chain came together. Eve was a student at Hampshire College and at Smith, and worked for Save the Children at a Women's Center in Songklah in Thailand. Margaret Chamberlain graduated from Smith, and also spent time in Southeast Asia. After her graduation she went to work for CWS in domestic resettlement in New York, and then became a resettlement officer with the Joint Voluntary Agency in Malaysia - working both in Kuala Lumpur and in Pilau Bidong. Margaret returned to the States last year, entered the Fletcher School of Law and Diplomacy at Tufts University and has just finished a Master's thesis called "Crisis Management and Refugee Movement". For the last two years Margaret has been my research assistant on the refugee project. It gives me special pleasure to invite her to chair the last session.

Margaret Chamberlain: It seems to me an overwhelming task to try to introduce the final session of our conference on "Working with Refugees", a conference that has been so interesting, that has brought up so many different points of view from people at such different levels. I am going to bring up a few very brief points - mainly focusing on prospects rather than on a retrospective of either the field or this conference.

Prospects and the future are rarely looked at in refugee work. There is rarely any long term view of international aspects of refugee work, or of the domestic side of things. In the international realm, in our sessions here, we have looked at protection, selection and admission, and Sheppie [Abramowitz] spoke of the situation in Thailand and of volunteerism. Lots of questions have been brought up about new catch-words, "development-oriented strategies", "the fluidity of international orders", "root-causes", etc. Old questions came up as well: questions of asylum, the parameters of international law, roles of international organizations. But perhaps even more important is what is going to be happening ten, twenty or thirty years down the line... .

As Michael Huynh said, when are refugees in this country no longer refugees? When will Americans accept the newcomers as part of their communities so that they can actually become that?

It seems to me that we sometimes make the mistake of seeing refugees as 'supermen' and 'superwomen'. We expect them to resettle anywhere. They can go to Belize even though no one else wants to be there. As David Pierce pointed out, it is not fair to place expectations on refugees we would not be able to hold for ourselves. There are so many mixed messages and misunderstandings going on in the field today.

I was told a story last year when I was doing some interviews for Peter Rose's Refugee Project that I thought really pointed out the complexities and confusions. The administrator of an agency told me that a federal agent had been visiting a certain state in the Northeast. He was berating the Mutual Assistance Association leaders because their members are a drain on the welfare system. An MAA leader stood up and said that while many people do think that he, for example, had made a certain number of dollars last year in his job as a case manager, and now found himself in a very high tax bracket and had to pay x-amount of taxes. At this point the federal official said to him, "Well that is just a different situation. Nobody should pay that amount of taxes. What you really need is a better tax lawyer." Really! What are we communicating to people?

With that thought I will turn this over to Dr. Charles Keely, a well known person in the field of refugee affairs and immigration matters. He is the Senior Associate of the Population Council in New York. Dr. Keely's research has focused on U.S. immigration policy, worker migration in the Middle East, and most recently on refugee policy. In addition to this research and to writing on international migration, Dr. Keely serves as Chairman of the Board of the National Forum on Immigration and Citizenship. He is also one of the foremost people in this field and someone to whom many graduate students such as I look to for information in his writings.

Charles Keely: At this moment, a Voyager spacecraft is journeying beyond our solar system. It contains a disk with the image of a man and woman and the location of our sun and planet. It also contains music. There is the hope that some person out there - for what else shall we call intelligent life but persons - will encounter the craft and recognize that we too are persons. We are also beginning a project to scan the skies - a search for extraterrestrial intelligence - to see if somebody had the same idea and sent us images and symbols that we can receive. I personally do not begrudge these efforts to probe and push back frontiers. But, be that as it may, I can not help to see the sad irony in the fumbling efforts to address global refugee problems while we send music to the stars and fumble with the dials on our cosmic "Walkman".

I am to provide a retrospect and a prospect. A retrospect can be quicksand, sucking us into a past that we cannot seem to transcend. A prospect can be an invitation to irresponsibility. What price does a forecaster pay if he is wrong? Usually none. That the "world will little note nor long remember what we say here" is the forecaster's shield and buckler.

To be asked to do a retrospect and a prospect is to be invited to be a prophet in the biblical sense: to discern the past, to read the signs of the times, and to propose a course of action that will make the future different, and better, than it would have been. But you, by your work with refugees, like it or not, are also to be prophets in the same sense. I use this religious image with no apology. To work on refugee issues, if we are the least bit serious, confronts us, as religious reflection does, with some basic issues: Who are we? How do we treat our fellow human beings? How do we build societies that respect and encourage our humanity? The Voyager spacecraft is even a religious act. It is a puff of mechanical incense sent, I suspect, not only with the hope of finding intelligent life but of finding intelligent life that has gone through what we are going through, has avoided self-annihilation, and can teach us to control our fears and destructiveness. In a sense, Voyager is a pilgrim in search of a teacher. We cannot wait for the pilgrim's return. Like any good prophet, we must be in the know. Our first message to one another is to take ourselves seriously. Do not become cogs in the welfarization of resettlement. Do not subordinate refugees to the interests of global politics. Man is the measure of societies and of governments and their policies. It is not the other way around. I know that may sound like I am preaching a crusade to Don Quixotes to fire you up for jousting with windmills. If you think that, you do not take yourself seriously. The issues surrounding refugees and the forces at work creating and responding to uprooted and persecuted people are no figments of the imagination.

What are those issues and forces at work? I will divide my remarks between the global situation and then focus on the United States.

The international edifice built to respond to refugees, while not in a shambles, at least has cracks in the foundation and structural flaws. Governments decide who to label as refugees. The criteria for who is and who is not a refugee and their applications are social creations. The definitions in the UN convention and protocol were developed in a European context to deal with the victims of international wars between developed countries. The political context of ideological differences made the labeling process relatively easy compared to the contemporary situation. Even if relief was not as forthcoming as some would have wanted, who were refugees in Europe was pretty clear, at least in the Western world.

Refugees today, by and large, are from and in developing countries as a result of civil wars and attempts at state and regime building. Refugees are primarily a development issue - in the sense of economic, social and political development of a nation state within the world system of states of today. The process of decolonization and the process of building nation states and incorporating them in a system of states are still unfinished processes. And these processes take place within a context, often violent, of competing ideologies on the nature and function of the government or state apparatus and its relationship to citizens. In almost every developing nation, regardless of prevailing ideology, the role of government in economic and even social life is pervasive. It now becomes more and more difficult to reach agreement on who is a refugee within the legal framework developed in the past. Take, for example, the Ghanian migrant workers, some of whom were there illegally, who were recently expelled from Nigeria. Some are referring to them as the refugees from Nigeria. Their circumstances in many respects are, in human terms, quite similar to refugees and Ghana is like a country of first asylum.

The UN definition of a refugee covers people who are persecuted and not those fleeing the general devastation of war, much less economic problems or even collapse. One need only think of Central America or Haiti to wonder whether, in human terms, the distinction is too much of a legal nicety.

One issue posed by those countries who accept refugees as an international responsibility and participate in international efforts to aid them, is how to preserve the special status of persons persecuted because of race, religion, national origin, membership in a particular social group or political opinion. I hold no brief that attempts to preserve that special status are made by those governments from the purest of humanitarian motives. Attempts to apply the definition in new contexts are running into resistance to say the least. Tactically, the attempts may backfire since the response may be not to broaden the application but to restrict it even further by placing a next to impossible burden of proof on applicants. This has taken place in a number of countries regarding asylum applications, although the UNHCR and the voluntary agencies have generally opted in the direction of humanitarian relief based on a broader interpretation of refugee and some would say are stretching it beyond credibility.

Once one gets into the details of going beyond immediate relief to issues of self-sufficiency while awaiting repatriation or integration into asylum countries, the problems become even thicker. They show up in jurisdictional squabbles about refugee versus development mandates and issues of funding. The need for development funding in refugee sending countries as a necessary ingredient for any hope of a permanent political solution permitting voluntary repatriation raises additional problems for the international community - or at least some of its members.

In retrospect, the current impasse on international response to refugees is the result of trying to adapt agreements and mechanisms designed in a different context to new realities. The UNHCR will not be made over into a development agency - although it has and I think will take on some of those functions. Nor, on the other hand, do I see the special status of the politically persecuted being given up and merged into a broader category of people needing relief from war, natural disaster or failures of development economics.

Prospectively, positive movement to break the current impasse can result if the concept of international responsibility is extended to include not only refugees in the classic sense, but to those innocent victims fleeing the devastation of war (civil or otherwise) and the innocent victims of failures in development. Such aid should not be seen as charity on the part of governments, but as a requirement of being a nation state and part of the system of nation states. Refugees were accepted as an international responsibility by many nations after World War I. It now must be recognized that achieving and maintaining the status of a nation state is not synonymous with declaring independence. Economic self-sufficiency is impossible for a nation to sustain for long in today's interdependent world. Economic viability is not synonymous with political sovereignty. If nations wish to have a system of nation states, they must take responsibility for the victims of that system. If we can do it for finance, can we not do it for people? Whether particular nations are or feel responsible for the conditions that lead to the production of a specific human tragedy, if they want to maintain any semblance of a stable world system, they must accept responsibility not in charity, but as a requirement of system maintenance.

I suspect that progress in that direction will be achieved not by trying to re-define refugees in international law, but by affirming that in addition to refugees - that is, in addition to the politically persecuted - there are other categories of people who must be seen as an international responsibility. Effort on their behalf cannot be seen as charity - and therefore dispensible - but as a requirement for maintaining any sort of stability in international relations be they political, trade, financial and, ultimately, peace itself.

Second, I think there needs to be more emphasis in international practice on solutions in place and less on permanent resettlement. I think too much lip service is given to repatriation as the preferred solution. It does not take a forecaster to predict that the bulk of today's refugees will not be permanently resettled in a third country. Not that there will not be some need of resettlement and that this could continue to involve large numbers of people at times. Those efforts, however, affect a small proportion of refugees. Time, effort and money go disproportionately for operations aimed at or part of resettlement. Until that is changed, I doubt that attention to solutions in place will be more vigorously pursued. The acceptance of international responsibility for victims beyond refugees will be resisted, and resisted at our peril.

Third, on a global level, there must be reaffirmation that granting asylum or refuge is not an unfriendly act between governments, but causing refugees is.

Mention of the legal tradition that granting asylum is not to be interpreted as an unfriendly act brings me to the United States. One characteristic of U.S refugee actions since the early 1950s has been to almost go out of our way to make admission of refugees a series of unfriendly acts by attempting to rub the noses of communists in the inferiority of their economic and political systems, as shown when people can vote with their feet. Is it any wonder, then, that the U.S. finds it so difficult to grant asylum to people from countries whose governments are, in diplomatic terms, friendly governments? While I can understand the dismay, there should be no shock that extended voluntary departure is currently selectively granted depending on whether the country of origin's government is communist or leaning toward communism.

Another characteristic of U.S. refugee activities is that we think of ourselves as a resettlement country. This has presented us with two problems; first we find it difficult, if not impossible, to think of ourselves - and perhaps for others to think of us - as a country of asylum, a temporary haven until voluntary repatriation is possible. We assume - and possibly quite rightly given past behavior - that, once here, asylees will not return. Second, I suspect that in our foreign policy we have acted first and thought of the refugee consequences later, almost as if there were a blank check for refugee resettlement in terms of both numbers and costs. For example, U.S. officials in Southeast Asia after the fall of Saigon have been accused of encouraging refugee movements from Vietnam partially in hopes of precipitating a predicted economic collapse by the loss of refugees' skills and talents. Whether true or not, such an accusation rests on the presumption that large scale resettlement in the U.S., integral to such a strategy, would not be a source of concern to those U.S. officials. I think that is a fair presumption about the state of things at the time. I wonder also to what extent the refugee generating possibilities of U.S. policy in Central America are even considered in foreign policy making. By refugee generation I have in mind not only movements to the U.S., but also stability considerations in the region and relations with Mexico. My main point with these examples is that the capacity for U.S. resettlement of refugees does have limits. I think those limits have not been seriously considered in foreign policy. On the contrary, they have been too much taken for granted. Now that the limits of resettlement are under question, I get the feeling that policy makers and others think that resettlement policy is coterminous with refugee policy.

In sum, our tradition as a resettlement country places limits on our ability to be a country of asylum and at least arguably has provided a safety value for foreign policy decisions that may go awry. One result is that the resettlement issue so fills the field of vision that other refugees are seen as marginal irritants in global or regional power politics.

In terms of resettlement in the U.S., no retrospective look can pass over the changes in resettlement practice begun with the Interagency Task Force developed for Indochinese resettlement and contained in the Refugee Act of 1980. The change in the definition of a refugee in U.S. law has not reduced the anti-communist bias by much nor reduced the ad hoc decision making of the past. The parole power of the Attorney General has been replaced by extended voluntary departure. The solid foundation for financing resettlement through the consultation process and legislative entitlements has been shifting, much to the dismay of state and local governments, and has been accompanied by dependency rates of real concern - even if exaggerated by statistical reporting methods. Resettlement has been set on a course of being a welfare function in the perjorative sense of that term. The role and functioning of the voluntary agencies in decision making and resettlement activities is in flux, to say the least. The private sector role, it is safe to say, will ultimately be much reduced. It is clear I am "underwhelmed" by the results of the last half dozen years in the resettlement side of U.S. policy, nor do I see the 1980 Refugee Act as any kind of breakthrough. To me it has been less of a landmark than a landmine.

What are the prospects? It is tempting to confine myself to prognosticating on the fate of the Simpson-Mazzoli Bill and the reauthorization of the Refugee Act. But my charge is to give a retrospect and prospect. I hope I am not dismissed as a mere grammarian if I pass over the opportunity of being a political tout by not giving you the prospects of legislation in the current session of Congress in favor of giving a prospect in the sense of a vision - or more modestly a few guidelines.

Those who work with refugees must be in the forefront of focusing the nation's vision on refugees throughout the world. It may mean you will work yourself out of a job or at least precipitate a career change to more overseas involvement. Permanent solutions and work in places of asylum must capture more of the world's and especially America's attention.

The fundamental problem of U.S. policy is not the definition of a refugee but its application. In my opinion, trying to redefine a refugee in legislation so as to reduce administrative discretion to a minimum will not aid the plight of refugees, or the victims of inhumanity on the battlefield or in the market place. Those who work with refugees can be a part of the foreign policy community or continue to clean up after it.

If the United States is to continue to accept refugees for resettlement, even if in reduced numbers, it behooves us all to pay attention to the fate of voluntary agencies. If resettlement becomes a largely state welfare function, the numbers will go down further than the need and the cost per capita to the public coffers will go up. Even if you have deep criticism of voluntary agencies, reformation is not destruction. Nor will the past return, but the private sector through its networks should not be lost to the integration process.

I also suggest that you look for opportunities, even in the most unlikely places. The individual review of asylum petitions is currently criticized as a thinly disguised method to reduce refugee flow and especially those from friendly governments like Haiti or El Salvador. If you agree and continue your efforts to have extended voluntary departure applied, do not overlook the possibility that the current policy lays the ground work for U.S. admission of asylees from friendly governments. The current image of the hard nosed, narrow, by-the-book review makes asylum as hard as the camel passing through the eye of the needle. Once established, that procedure may well serve to allow the U.S. to accept and present to others that asylum is not an unfriendly act by the U.S., no matter what the origin. Some may be saved who otherwise would not. I do not suggest this as a slap in the face of current frustrations, but do not lose any opportunity to save the victims you serve. Once the hard nosed image of individual review is established, relaxation in the application of criteria can provide a welcome avenue for a considerably larger number of admissions.

I realize I have not presented an agenda for action to loosen up Indochinese movements, or a strategy on the first asylum issue, or a plan of action for structuring domestic resettlement. I have not even said whether I would suggest optimism or pessimism about the 1983 congressional session. I have no stirring call for action nor picture of despair to confirm any tendencies you have to blame those evil people in Washington or parts of the American public for their inhumanity and blindness in the face of suffering.

You have to supply those things. You have to work out the specifics, the items on agendas, the details of programs, the coordination of mandates, and your own optimism or pessimism. You surely will have failure and face bitter frustrations, as well as triumphs of sorts. I only offer you this one speculation for those among you who serve refugees. If you take yourself seriously and continue your work, I suspect that if Voyager does make contact and intelligent life comes here - people whose civilizations have gone through what we humans do to one another and have survived - I think those visitors, those teachers, may want to talk to you and the refugees before they talk to the politicians and to the generals or even to Carl Sagan.

Peter Rose: Thank you Charlie - and all of you - for being with us, urging us to reflect on matters of utmost importance, and helping us to remember the life and spirit of Simon Shargo, refugee worker and citizen of the world.

INDEX

Abramowitz, M., ix, 74, 75, 78, 81
Abramowitz, S., ix, xii, 2, 27, 74-75, 81, 93, 94, 95, 100, 101
Abrams, E., 30
Afghanistan (Afghans), 4, 5, 8, 26, 40, 60
Africa, 2, 4, 5, 6, 11, 13, 19, 22, 27, 37, 60, 78, 92
Agency for International Development (AID), 80
Aid to Families and Dependent Children (AFDC), 84
Alien Rights Law Group, 38
American Council of Nationalities Services, xiii, 94
American Council of Voluntary Agencies for Foreign Service, 3
American Emergency Relief Administration, 72
American Jewish Committee, 94
American Jewish Joint Distribution Committee (AJJDC), x, 2, 73, 75
American Relief Administration, x
Annual Refugee Number Review, 80
Antigua, 32
Argentina, 36
Arizona, 86
Asia (Asians), 6, 11, 16, 27, 37, 66
Australia, 6, 16, 24

Bangkok, 54, 57
Bangladesh, 21
Belize, 24, 102
Bengalis, 27
Berlin, x, 73
Boston, MA, 91, 94
Brainerd, G.S., xii, 44, 47, 51, 54, 56, 57, 58, 60
Brown, M., 76

Brown, R., xii, 92, 93, 95
Buddhism, 67
Burton, E., 70, 101
Burundi, 26

California, 15, 17, 30,·32, 54, 55, 69, 74, 90, 96
Cambodia (Cambodians), 5, 6, 7, 10, 13, 14, 22, 26, 48, 55, 68, 69, 74, 75, 77, 79, 82, 93, 94
Cameroon, 4
Camus, A., 9
Canada, 6, 24, 26
Caribbean, 22
Carter, J., 33, 87
Catholic Community Services, Inc., xiii, 84
Center for Southeast Asian Refugee Resettlement, xii, 65
Central America, 11, 22, 78, 104, 106
Central Valley of California, 92
Chad, 4-5
Chamberlain, M.D., xii, 101
Cherne, L., 100
Chicago, 35
Child Welfare League of America, 84, 86
Chile (Chileans), 16, 37
China (Chinese), 93
Chinese Exclusion Act, 33, 93
Church World Service, ix, xii, xiii, 3, 54, 90, 91
Colorado, 90
Committee of Migration and Refugee Affairs, 3
Conventional Arms Talks, ix, 75
Conway, J.K., ix, xii, 1
Council on Accreditation, 84, 86
Cuba (Cubans), 6, 13, 15, 22, 35, 36, 38, 84, 85, 87, 96

Cypress, 4

DeHaan, D., ix, xii, 2-3, 10, 18, 35, 60, 78
DeVecchi, R., xii, 10, 21, 23, 25, 57, 59, 67, 74, 98
Delhi Agreement, 21
Department of Human Resources, Portland, OR, xiii
Department of Social Services, New York City, 59
Displaced Persons, 11, 19, 23, 31, 73
Djiboti, 4

Early Warning Systems, 26
Eastern Europeans, 35
Ecumenical Refugee Resettlement and Sponsorship Services, 90
Eglin Air Force Base, 17
Einstein, A., 21
El Salvador (Salvadorians), 4, 5, 8, 22, 26, 30, 36, 37, 38, 40, 41, 42, 86, 107
Emergency Rescue Committee, 21
English as a Second Language (ESL) Training, 17, 46, 47, 56, 58, 71, 92
Eritria, 26
Ethiopia (Ethiopians), 4, 5, 8, 28

Family Liaison Unit, ix, xii
Family Service Association, 86
Federation of Jewish Philanthropies of N.Y., xiii, 52, 62
Fletcher School of Law and Diplomacy, xii, 101
Florida, 33, 42, 84
Forbes, S., xii, 83, 87, 90, 94, 97, 98
Ford, D., xii
Ford, G., 87
Fort Chaffee, 17
Fort Indiantowngap, 17
Fort McCoy, 17
Fortune, 85
France, 24, 57
Free University of Amsterdam, 2
Fresno, CA, 92
Friedline, M., xii, 44, 56, 58, 91

Galang, 25
Geneva, x, 2, 73, 100
Geneva Convention, 19
Georgetown, 2
Georgia, 63
Germany, x, 21, 73
Ghana (Ghanians), 104
Global Refugee Policy, x
Gordenker, L., xii, 10, 12, 15, 17, 21, 23, 28
Guatemala, 4, 37, 41, 42

Haiti (Haitians), 8, 22, 30, 33, 34, 36, 37, 38, 40, 41, 42, 104, 107
Haitian Refugee Center, 43
Haitian Refugee Center v. Civiletti, 39
Havana, 16
Hebrew Immigrant Aid Society (H.I.A.S.), xiii, 52, 58, 74
Hitler, A., 21
Hmien, 49, 54
Hmong, 49, 51, 54, 92
Honduras, 4, 37, 76
Hong Kong, 16, 25, 26, 33, 41, 74, 93
Hoover, H., x, 72
Hoyt, N.S., x, 1, 73
Hungarian Freedom Fighters, 85
Hungary (Hungarians), 16
Huynh, M., xii, 65, 67, 69, 102

Idaho, 90
Illegal Aliens, 18, 19
Immigration and Naturalization Service (INS), 29, 37, 38, 57, 79, 86
Imperial Valley, CA, 32
Indochina (Indochinese), 13, 24, 25, 26, 30, 35, 37, 40, 44, 45, 59, 62, 74, 78, 87, 88
Institute of Human Relations, 94
Intergovernmental Committee for Migration, xii, xiii, 15, 44
International Committee for the Red Cross (ICRC), 14, 15, 79
International Committee on Migration (ICM), 15, 16, 17, 22, 24, 70, 100
International Red Cross, 19
International Rescue Committee (IRC), xii, 21, 70, 74, 75,
Involuntary Repatriation, 14
Iran, 4, 38
Iraq, 4
Ireland (Irish), 43
Israel, 73

Jews, x, 72
Joint Voluntary Agency, xiii, 54, 74, 101
Jordan, C., 73

Kampala, 25
Kampuchea (Kampucheans), 5, 21, 26
Keely, C.B., x, xiii, 102
Kennedy, T., 2
Key West, FL, 17
Keynes, 34
Khmer, 6, 13, 14, 15, 70, 76, 78, 79
Khmer Emergency Group, ix, xii, 74, 75
King, Judge, 34
Kousseri, 4-5

INDEX

Kuala Lumpur, 101

Laos (Laotians), 6, 19, 54
Latin America, 11, 36, 37
Lawyers Committee for Human Rights, xiii, 35
Lazarus, E., 30
Lebanon, 4, 16, 19
"Limits of Cultural Pluralism" (The), 43
Los Angeles, CA, 17, 30, 32, 91
Los Angeles Refugee Forum, xii, 44
Lowell, R., 6
Lutherans, 86
Lutheran Immigration and Refugee Service, xii, 68
Lutheran Service Association, xiii, 67, 93
Lutheran Social Services, 92

Malaysia, 4, 6, 16, 21, 25
Manila, 57
Mariel boatlift, 16-17, 22, 84, 85
Marseilles, 73
Massachusetts, 3, 96
Mazzoli, R.L., 29, 42, 43
McCarren-Walter Act, 35, 37
Mencken, H.L., 59
Merced, CA, 92
Mexico (Mexicans), 32, 40, 106
Miami, FL, xiii, 17, 22, 84, 85, 96
Michigan State University, xiii, 10
Middle East, 60, 92
Migration and Refugee Service (USCC), ix, xii, xiii
Milwaukee, 86
Muskie, E., 74

Namibia, 4
National Association of Evangelicals, 44
National Conference of Catholic Charities, 84, 86
National Forum on Immigration and Citizenship, 102
National Immigration, Refugee and Citizenship Forum, xiii, 39
National Jewish Agencies, 86
National Security Council, 39
National Volunteer Week, 75
Ndjamena, 4-5
Nevada, 90, 91
New England, 68, 93, 94, 98
New England Khmer Studies Institute, 68
New Orleans, 88
"New Orleans Seeks To Halt New Cuban Refugee Project", 88
New York City, 17, 43, 63, 64, 71

New Zealand, 24
Newman, S., xiii, 62, 65, 71
Nicaragua, 4, 38
Nicoliev, x, 72
Nigeria, 4, 19, 104
Nigerian Civil War, 6
Nkomo, J., 11
Non-refoulement, 13
North Vietnam, 19
Northampton, MA, x, 2

Odessa, x
Office of Refugee Resettlement, 57-58
Orange County Register (The), 88
Orange County, CA, xii, xiii, 30-31, 44, 87, 89, 91, 97
Orderly Departure Program, 57
Oregon State Department of Adult and Family Services, 47
Oregon, 50

Pacific Asian Consortium for Employment, 15
Pacific-American Consortium for Employment, xiii
Pakistan (Pakistani), 2, 4, 5, 8, 17, 26, 27, 37, 38
Pakistani Civil War, 6
Palestine (Palestinians), 5, 16, 23, 34
Paris, x, 73
Pathet Lao, 19
Peace Corps, 30, 89
People's Republic of China, 16, 26
Perry, 65
Philippines, 4, 16, 25, 37, 38, 71
Pierce, D., xiii, 30, 34, 35, 39, 40, 41, 43, 87, 90, 96, 97, 102
Pilau Bidong, 101
Pol Pot, 69
Poland (Poles), 4, 8, 38, 60
Pond, P., xiii, 67, 70, 78, 93, 94, 95
Population Council, x, xiii, 102
Portland, OR, xiii
Portland Area Refugee Service Consortium, xiii, 48,
Posner, M., xiii, 35, 38, 39, 40, 42, 51
Princeton University, xii, 10
Providence, RI, 94
Pullen, J., xiii, 47, 56, 60

Rand Corporation, 41
Reagan, R., 75, 87
Refoulement, 20
Refugee Act of 1980, 2, 35, 40, 41, 42, 55, 83, 106, 107

Repatriation, 5-6, 11. 14, 20, 44
Resource Development Department, xiii
"Retrospect and Prospect", x
Refugee Policy Group (RPG), xii, xiii, 12, 13, 42, 83
Rhode Island University, xiii
Risvi, Z., xiii, 17, 24, 26, 69, 74
Rodino, P.W., 43
Rome, 17, 100
Roosevelt, E., 21
Rose, P.I., xiii, 1, 9, 71, 72, 81, 100, 102, 108
Rosenblatt, L., xiii, 12, 22, 24, 26, 27, 74, 77
Ruanda (Ruandans), 25, 26, 27
Rubin, G., xiii, 94, 95, 98
Rustin, B., 2, 70

S.S. St. Louis, 73
Sacramento, CA, 92
Sage, B., xiii, 54, 57, 74
Sakaeo, 69
San Diego, CA, 30, 91
San Francisco, CA, xii, 65, 69, 91
San Francisco Refugee Forum, 65, 90
Sanctuary, 86-87
Santa Ana, CA, 13, 32
Save the Boat People, 48
Save the Children, 101
Schroeder, M., xiii, 61, 65, 67, 69, 70, 71
Seattle, WA, 86
Sentimental Imperialists (The), 65
Shargo, S., x-xi, 22, 72-74, 75, 81, 100, 108
Siberia, 73
Simpson, A.K., 12, 29, 42
Simpson-Mazzoli Bill, 39, 80, 107
Smith College, xiii
Smith College Study of Refugees, xii
Social Security, 45
Socialist Revolutionary Party, 73
Somalia, 4, 5
Songklah, 101
South Africans, 8
South Korea, 38
South Vietnam, 19
Southeast Asia, 2, 4, 8, 12, 15, 19, 25, 41, 100, 106
Soviet Jewish Program, 63
Soviet Jewish Resettlement Programs in U.S., xiii
Soviet Jews, 8, 36, 52, 62, 64, 71
St. Paul, MN, 13
Stanley, 65
State Refugee Coordinator, Oregon, 51
Stein, B., xiii, 10, 22, 23, 100, 101
Stockton, CA, 92
Sudan (Sudanese), 4, 5, 21, 26
Swartz, D.F., xiii, 22, 38, 39, 78
Sweden (Swedes), 33

Tel Aviv, 100
Temporary Foreign Workers, 39-40
Thai Committee for Refugees, 67
Thailand (Thais), ix, xii, 5, 7, 12, 14, 15, 16, 21, 25, 26, 27, 33, 54, 57, 68, 70, 74, 75, 77, 78, 79, 94, 101
Thompson, 65
Toffler, A., 34
Tufts University, xii

Uganda, 4, 16, 19, 25, 27
Ukraine, x, 72
Una Chapman Cox Sabbatical Program, xiii, 12
Union of Soviet Socialist Republics (Soviets), 2, 4, 26, 53, 59, 62, 63, 64, 71, 72
United Church of Christ, 67
United Jewish Appeal (U.J.A.), 53
United Nations, 2, 3, 5, 6, 7, 18, 20, 27, 35, 100, 104
United Nations Convention Relating to the Status of Refugees, 18, 35
United Nations High Commissioner for Refugees (UNHCR), ix, xii, xiii, 5, 7, 13, 14, 15, 16, 17, 20, 25, 26, 37, 38, 74, 79, 80, 104
United Nations International Children's Education Fund (UNICEF), 14, 15
United Nations Protocol, 40
United Nations Relief and Rehabilitation Administration, 23
United Nations Relief Works Agency (UNRWA), 23
United Nations Security Council, 23
United Presbyterian Church, 90
United States Catholic Conference, xiii, 70
United States Catholic Conference, Migration and Refugee Services, xiii, 84
United States Department of Defense, 80
United States Department of Health and Human Services (HHS), 57, 59
United States Department of State, ix, xii, 12, 29, 37, 38, 39, 57, 75
United States Foreign Service, xii, xiii, 21, 30, 87
United States Interagency Task Force, 106
University in Exile, 21

Vann, 101
Vienna, ix, 53, 75, 100
Vietnam (Vietnamese), 5, 6, 55, 69, 70, 101, 106

Walsh, B., xiii, 21, 42, 84, 89
Waltermire, P., xiii, 90, 95, 96
Washington, DC, 57

Weizmann, C., 34
Western Massachusetts Cambodian Foster
  Children Program, 92
What Color is Your Parachute?, 90
White Russians, 16
Wilson, H., 18
World Bank, 11
World Relief, xii, 44
World War I, 104
World War II, 7, 18, 19, 23, 27, 29, 37, 63

YMCA, 88

Zaire, 28
Ziebert, R., xiii, 15, 25
Zimbabwe, 5, 11, 24
Zionism, 73
Zucker, N., xiii, 29, 34, 35, 38, 43
Zukerman, K.D., xiii, 52, 56, 58, 63, 74